Edgar Cayce always saw each person as a unit of energy in the earth, a creation of Universal Forces which we call God, an entity who is distinct from every other being on the face of the earth, and who deserves to be treated as such. Thus his suggestions were always a bit different for each seeker who came to him for help.

Cayce saw each man, woman, or child as an eternal being born again into the earth each time with a purpose. His readings encompassed this concept of reincarnation, or the continuity of life from the point of creation (perhaps millions of years ago) up to the present moment.

One's life purpose was often pointed out, even while offering a diet to help the body recover a better state of health. For he recalled to mind frequently the concept that God was indeed our Source—and our life here on planet Earth is an opportunity to make headway back to that Source, which is our rightful destiny.

✳

Edgar Cayce
on
Healing Foods

FOR
BODY, MIND
AND SPIRIT

✳

William A. McGarey, M.D.

BANTAM BOOKS
NEW YORK · TORONTO · LONDON · SYDNEY · AUCKLAND

EDGAR CAYCE ON HEALING FOODS
A Bantam Book/November 1989

ISBN 0-553-28327-8

Published simultaneously in the United States and Canada

Bantam Books are published by Bantam Books, a division of
Bantam Doubleday Dell Publishing Group, Inc. Its trademark,
consisting of the words ''Bantam Books'' and the portrayal of a
rooster, is Registered in U.S. Patent and Trademark Office and in
other countries. Marca Registrada. Bantam Books, 666 Fifth
Avenue, New York, New York 10103

PRINTED IN THE UNITED STATES OF AMERICA

OPM 0 9 8 7 6 5 4 3 2 1

DEDICATION

This book is dedicated to two people who, aside from Edgar Cayce (the man who gave the readings), were most important in making this information from the readings available to the world as a whole:

Hugh Lynn Cayce—Edgar's son
and
Gladys Davis Turner—Edgar's secretary

They, like Edgar, have moved on to another dimension, but their reality and the good that they did does indeed live on.

WILLIAM A. MCGAREY, M.D.

ACKNOWLEDGMENTS

There are many efforts that go into making a book. This is especially true with this endeavor, since I am more of an expert on the Edgar Cayce psychic data than I am on diets, especially cooking and preparing them.

Without the expert advice and guidance of June Newton, much information in this book would be lacking. June is the gourmet chef, as she likes to call herself, for our Temple Beautiful Program, and if you were to see the table when dinner is ready to go, you would understand why. Also, I would be remiss if I didn't recognize the expertise that Erika Bauer has added to how one understands the Cayce readings about diet. These are the real experts. I am, in a real sense, just the reporter. Peggy Grady, the assistant director of our 17-day Temple Beautiful Program from its beginning, has added comment, perspective, recipes, and help.

This book has been a long time in the making. The Victoria, Australia, *Search for God Study Group Newsletter* has given its bit of help, although those who edited it may not even know how. The A.R.E. (Association for Research and Enlightenment) library staff, Mae Gimbert St. Clair, Marilyn Petersen, and all those who work with the readings in any way have contributed in many ways to the essence of this work. Meredith Puryear, in her selection of readings for meetings that I have taken part in at Virginia Beach, Virginia, has contributed.

Here at the clinic, my wife, Gladys, has always been supportive in urging me onward and taking up the work slack when I've been gone. Our six progeny have given both of us lessons in how to practice common sense in our eating habits, and Gladys has several delicious recipes in that section of this book.

And, in our study group activities, Anne Read, through her comments and the book she co-authored (see Bibliography), brought diet and eating habits to our attention constantly and productively.

Without Maxine Aten's proficiency and talent at her secretarial art, my putting things together would have floundered. Many have volunteered their help in one way or another, and I owe thanks to a host of unnamed assistants.

WILLIAM A. MCGAREY, M.D.
A.R.E. Clinic, Inc.
Phoenix, Arizona

CONTENTS

Contents

Contents

PREFACE

About two-thirds of the psychic readings that my grandfather, Edgar Cayce, gave during his lifetime were in response to individuals' questions about health and healing. Most of the total of some 14,500 stenographically recorded discourses given in an unconscious trance state have been indexed by subject, including those on health-related subjects. Edgar Cayce died in 1945, but now we ask, how helpful today is that information, given for individuals years ago? The author of this book, William McGarey, has taken the lead in trying to answer that question related to the health ideas in the Edgar Cayce readings. Bill and his wife, Gladys, both medical doctors, have been pioneers both in studying and testing the principles of diet and nutrition in this book and in leading the medical community to a closer look at the relationships between body, mind, and spirit as they influence our health.

All of us are aware of how our diet can affect how we feel. We need only reflect on the effect of an alcoholic drink or a cup of coffee, or that feeling after a big Thanksgiving dinner. Our society is also becoming more aware of the more complex and longer-term effects of our diet. I recently read in *Newsweek* a cover article about the relationship of nutrition to levels of stress, and there are thousands of such articles. One only need watch our national best-seller lists to see a reflection of our concern about this aspect of our lives. There are dietary and nutrition principles in the Cayce readings that are now being confirmed as important general principles for many of us to consider.

Bill McGarey has been studying these principles in the Edgar Cayce readings for over thirty-three years. He has tested them with his thousands of patients. He uses them himself. He has compared them with current medical research. He is especially qualified to share them. I encourage you to have a look and try them for yourself.

CHARLES THOMAS CAYCE, Ph.D.
President, A.R.E., Inc.

INTRODUCTION

Since Edgar Cayce's death in 1945, literally hundreds of books have been written about subjects discussed in his "readings"—and several tell about diet and health in one way or another. So, why another book?

Perhaps the best answer comes from my conviction that health is built on a foundation of what we eat, what we think, what we believe, and what we put into action by choice. I've found in my study of the Cayce material that the kind of physical and mental health we all have a right to enjoy cannot really happen unless we discover—and then make practical in our lives—the diet that is "right" for each one of us. And that, to me, is plain common sense.

In a letter Edgar Cayce wrote to a man who had obtained a reading (567–2), Cayce said, "Unless this information in the readings is plain common sense, we can't make it very practical."

The wealth of information in the Cayce readings has never before been explored in-depth to put together the concepts of healing, the manners in which food should be approached and used, and the powers of the mind and the spirit as they fashion this amazing creation we call the human body.

The purpose of this book is not to encompass all the above; rather, it is to add to the written literature another viewpoint of the wonders that can be found in your diet, the benefits that come about when you understand your body better, and the difficulties and roadblocks that may appear as you try to do just that and to make all of this as practical as possible.

Edgar Cayce left behind a legacy of psychic readings given from a state of extended consciousness. Two-thirds of these, resulting from individual requests, dealt with illnesses of the body and what might be done to correct them and restore the body back to a state of health.

As he looked at these bodies and the illnesses they were creating, Cayce talked about assimilations and eliminations, acid-alkaline balance, incoordinations, functions, relationships of one system or organ to another, and about disease resulting from disturbances in these kinds of physiological activities.

And, throughout his suggestions on ways to correct these conditions, he spoke volumes about diet. He saw certain food combinations as helpful, some as harmful. His theme throughout the readings was *Keep the body and its functions balanced,* often by using nutrition.

In the physical readings, Cayce recalled to readers the overall concept of the spiritual nature of the human being. "The spirit is the life," he often stated, "the mind is the builder and the physical is the result."

True healing of the body is an attunement of the physical and the mental to their spiritual source. When such a concept is brought into relationship with what we eat, we find a more special meaning in the kind of a diet we choose from day to day.

To one person (2265–1), Cayce suggested, "The diet should be not much meats. Fish or fowl may be eaten. As much green vegetable matter as may be taken. The body is very good in its mental abilities, and in the ability to give dietetics for *others*. Apply same then in self. Be consistent with every condition as goes to make up the physical, mental, and spiritual being. Do that."

One of my patients recently followed similar suggestions and dropped twenty pounds in six weeks from a body weight that needed desperately to be lowered.

To another who was asking advice (3051–6), Cayce suggested ". . . a well balanced diet. But often use the raw vegetables which are prepared with gelatin. Use these at least three times each week. Those which grow more above the ground than those which grow below the ground. Do include, when these are prepared, carrots with that portion especially close to the top. It may appear the harder and the less desirable but it carries the vital energies, stimulating the optic reactions between kidneys and the optics."

Cayce's suggestions about diet ranged from the spiritual quest to carrot tops—from the sublime to the ridiculous, in a sense. But always he saw each person as a unit of energy in the earth, a creation of Universal Forces which we call God, an entity who is distinct from every other being on the face of the earth, and who deserves to be treated as such. Thus his suggestions were always a bit different for each seeker who came to him for help.

Cayce saw each man, woman, or child as an eternal being born again into the earth each time with a purpose. His readings encompassed this concept of reincarnation, or the continuity of life from the point of creation (perhaps millions of years ago) up to the present moment.

One's life purpose was often pointed out, even while offering a diet to help the body recover a better state of health. For he recalled to mind frequently the concept that God was indeed our Source—and our life here on planet Earth is an opportunity to make headway back to that Source, which is our rightful destiny.

To a woman who sought physical help, Cayce gave this spiritual advice plus a deeper understanding of what her purpose really was in being born this lifetime:

> . . . Each *entity* is a universe, or a combination of universes, within itself. These reactions may depend upon the creative force within itself to carry on to the fulfillment of its purpose in any material experience.
>
> Do not *allow*, do not entertain any lack of confidence in self to contact the

creative energies within self sufficient for the fulfilling of that purpose.

Do these things materially. And . . . *meditate.*

Meditation means, then, the entering within self to seek for the Creative Forces; or to seek that God may make for the using of the body—mentally, physically, spiritually—as a greater manifestation of His love in and among men.

1020–1

Thus, to clarify the purpose of this book, it would be well to say that it is intended to give you a useful and practical source of information regarding what constructive eating is all about. From a commonsense point of view, it is written especially for those who are interested in seeking out their life purpose, in making a unique diet for themselves as unique individuals that will aid in maintaining health and assist in overcoming whatever may befall them as illnesses.

In the process, I hope to give you some concept of the importance of stress, attitudes, emotions, beliefs, habits, prayer, and meditation as they affect the use of food and your general health. A glossary in the back of the book will help define certain words or ideas. Have fun reading these pages. They will let you know that you are indeed incomparable in this universe—and that simply no one will need exactly the same kind of diet for full health as you do. Thus, you can be very creative as you search for that diet that will suit you best. And you can be assured that you can do it, you can find it. So, on with the search!

1

❋

MY SEARCH FOR GOOD NUTRITION

Good nutrition—a constructive diet that we might follow—becomes for many of us the open door to a new awareness, the beginning of a major change in consciousness.

Simply recognizing that the body has the ability to create within us life-giving substances out of those foods we put into our mouths is a revelation. For me it was. And that revelation, although slow in coming, brought me face-to-face with a concept I had read in the Bible and heard repeated literally hundreds of times: The body is indeed "the temple of the Living God."

As I came to the point of recognizing that the adoption of good dietary habits helped me in fashioning my own temple, I realized that this would give me insights into my spiritual reality and would open the door to those changes that bring more and greater spiritual growth.

As a child, my concern was not the kind of food I should or could eat, but rather—at least during those depression years—*would* there be food to eat? One of my most vivid childhood memories is of a trip I took in Wellsville, Ohio, me pulling my little wagon along with my father down the back alleys to the 12th Street storehouse where food was being given out to those who were in need. I didn't understand what was happening, but I knew that we stood in line for a long time, until Dad signed some papers and got a supply of food.

My mother had died in 1927, two years before the stock market crash that launched the Great Depression. Then Dad lost his job when the steel mill closed. He had to feed my two brothers and me, as well as himself, with no wages coming in. So we ate whatever we could get. If it didn't build our health, at least we didn't starve.

My wife, Gladys, also a medical doctor, and my partner through forty years of medical practice (while raising six children), had much the same kind of childhood. She also ate what she was given during those depression years. Her birth to missionary parents in India prepared her for a diet that was not the best—but it was always accompanied by prayer, and I'm sure that had a major effect on the benefits derived from the food.

During my teens, I recall celebrating my team's baseball victory with Pepsi-Colas—and I could down the entire bottle on occasion without stopping, not the best thing for my health. It seems that the human body has a tremendous ability to survive and stay relatively healthy under the most adverse circumstances. My teeth suffered, however, requiring some thirty fillings when I was just fifteen.

2

Today, our six grown children have a minimum of fillings. I would guess that together they
have not totaled in their lives the number of fillings
I had done that year when I was in my mid-teens.
Their diet, of course, has been totally different.
And that has made a great difference, not only in
their teeth but in their overall health.

Through my final years of high school and
college, I didn't think about my diet. It was only
when I got into medical school that the subject of
vitamins became part of my studies. Those years
(1943–7) were discovery years in the field of vitamins, but their use in medicine was almost non-
existent.

The subject fascinated me, however. I simplified the problem somewhat, figuring that if (1) the
lack of vitamins can cause scurvy and other recognized diseases, then (2) the use of vitamins
must relieve a variety of diseases where vitamins
might be in inadequate supply.

It seemed logical to me at that point in my
medical education that a human body receiving
an adequate supply of vitamins would very naturally be in a better state of health than one in
which the vitamins were lacking.

Surprisingly, this concept was not particularly
acceptable among the majority of my professors or
fellow students. It was apparent that the disease—
rather than the nutritional status of the patient—
was the focus of the studies, laboratory tests, X
rays, medical histories, and examinations. My interest, then, remained an interest only, and I had
little chance to try out my ideas, except on myself.
Vitamins did, however, enhance my state of
health—more energy, fewer colds. I simply felt bet-

3

ter. I still didn't know too much about nutrition or diets, but I had made the first step.

The attitude taken by medical schools in those days (which to a great extent still exists) was that nutrition had little, if any, importance; that the mind and the emotions had no direct, or even indirect effect on the physical body; that prayer was in no manner associated with the health of the body or with the correction of disease; and that meditation ("What's that?") would only be found in some of those strange Eastern religions. In my years at the University of Cincinnati, the mention of a Divine Being or God came about only in the profanity of the professors, residents, interns, and students. And, as for the subject of reincarnation, well . . . that wasn't even considered.

While there was little development toward an understanding of good nutrition during those days of my formal medical training, ideas about food gradually came into focus during the early years of my practice in the field of what is now called family medicine. From a state of what I call unawareness, I moved, step-by-step, into a sometimes painful awakening.

A woman patient of mine in Wellsville, where Gladys and I began our practice of medicine, was bedfast and not doing well due to an illness that was not readily diagnosable. From my interest in vitamins and the availability of injectable vitamin B-12, I gave this lady three consecutive daily injections of B-12. She was not only out of bed, but was moving around normally once again in a matter of just a few days.

Some years later, when I spent two years as a flight surgeon in the Air Force, I had many an argument with another medical officer who was trained in internal medicine. He could not see the benefit of B-12 for anything except pernicious anemia. Perhaps it was because he was so immersed in looking at the disease—was it treatable?—rather than the idea that the patient might be deficient in that particular vitamin without necessarily suffering from pernicious anemia. Early in my experience in the field of medicine, this reluctance to understand the importance of vitamins was the norm. In later years, I have found that there is a change coming about, slow as it seems in making its appearance.

Things had not improved to any extent in the late fifties or early sixties. I brought a case before a panel of physicians who were looking at problems in the Medicare coverage. The system had refused to pay for injectable vitamins for a patient who had a textbook case of vitamin deficiency and did not respond to oral dosages. I even took the textbook down to the meeting to show the doctors. They still could not understand what to me was obvious: The patient had not responded to oral vitamin therapy and needed (and responded to) the injectable form.

Gladys and I tried to use what knowledge we had of nutrition with our family. I will never forget the picture of our four-year-old Annie standing on the street near the ice-cream wagon, yelling so that everyone would hear her, "Everyone in the whole world gets ice cream except the McGareys!"

Nutrition was also important in our medical

practice. We came across the Koch cancer therapy not long after we opened our offices. Dr. William Koch had developed a substance he described as an oxidation catalyst. Although he had many adherents, Koch was eventually discredited by the established authorities in his attempts to treat cancer. One thing stood out among all other factors, however, in the regimen of therapy he prescribed. Eat a very good diet, no fried foods, lots of greens, don't cook with aluminum, drink lots of water—advice Edgar Cayce also put forth in his readings.

We adopted some of those ideas, although at that time we had no idea why such a diet would influence the course of a disease like cancer. But it did emphasize to me that it was important for all of us to adopt a diet that had in it all that the body needs. We wanted to keep ourselves and our patients from becoming deficient in the supply of body nutrients—and vitamins are some of those nutrients.

And I found that we can truly change our eating habits. If we dislike something, we can—with practice and the right attitude—learn to like it. I proved this for myself while in the Air Force. At the Officers' Club they served shrimp as hors d'oeuvres nearly every evening. I had never in my life even faintly liked shrimp. But I saw these people consuming shrimp like it was going out of style. I finally realized I must be missing something. So I decided to make a sincere effort to eat some shrimp and taste it very carefully, without my former prejudice. After just a few boiled shrimp taken gingerly, I was convinced, then ate more and more, and I found that I could overcome a distaste for certain foods if I tried.

Some years ago a woman patient of ours who had scleroderma went on a very clearly defined diet, eliminating pork products, among others. Some three years after that, free of the sclero-derma, she visited her mother, who wanted to know, "What can you eat now?" The answer came back, "I can eat anything I like!" Her mother served ham that night, and was rebuffed when the woman didn't eat any. "But you said you could eat anything you like!" The answer came back, "That's right, but now I don't *like* ham!"

It was after our family relocated and estab-lished our base in Phoenix, Arizona, in 1955 that we learned of Edgar Cayce. A whole new world opened for me. Not only did Cayce teach me about diet and nutrition, but he also introduced me to the concept of reincarnation. Understanding that concept, I no longer find it strange to realize that I am a continuing spiritual being moving through time and space, appearing here at this time, but having had lifetimes in the past that helped to create attitudes and emotional reactions that helped chart the course of life I am taking this time around.

This helped me look at the whole human being as the center of my attention as I practiced medi-cine, and it moved me away from the concept of being only a specialist in the diseases that attack the body. This represented a drastic change in my thinking. Care for the body *properly* . . . and the body becomes normal. A normal body has no dis-eases. So why not direct our efforts to normalizing the body? It fascinated me as I realized that I had rediscovered an ancient truth that had once been mine in previous incarnations.

Late in the 1950s, we had adopted the practice of using only whole wheat bread. A friend had told us about the only place he knew where real whole wheat bread was available. Stoll's Bakery was run by Mormons, who years ago recognized the value of whole wheat over the white, degerminated flour. It became a place we visited weekly. We would buy twelve to sixteen loaves to freeze and use for our growing family of six. In all of metropolitan Phoenix, this was the only place where we could find good, wholesome, naturally prepared whole grain bread.

At that point we took up one of our minor crusades—to make whole wheat bread more available for our patients and others throughout the Valley of the Sun. Each of our patients were given the same instructions: "Tell the manager or the check-out person at the grocery store you go to that you want some good whole wheat bread. And, if they don't supply it for you, that you'll go to another store." Most store managers want to meet the desires of their customers, so gradually it happened. Today it would be difficult to find any food store in Arizona that does not stock on its shelves a good supply of whole wheat bread.

It was nearly thirty years ago that Gladys and I entertained a professor of Harvard Medical School in our home when he visited Phoenix to speak to a medical society about nutrition. He was a fellow faculty member with Gladys's brother, Carl Taylor, and so we thought we had something in common. But we found he had no patience with what we were trying to do with good nutrition. Rather, he was an advocate of white flour products. These, he said, were well supplied with vitamins and were beneficial to health. His mini-crusade—which failed—was to get rid of health food stores.

Much has changed during the intervening years. Health food stores have flourished. Even the supermarkets put health foods on their shelves, provide good whole wheat bread, and sometimes have special health food sections.

More important than that, however, to me in my own practice of medicine, has been the growth of my own understanding of the nature of the human body—the variety of ways in which it works, which I learned from the Edgar Cayce readings.

I realized from the Edgar Cayce readings, for instance, that biochemically the body must have a stable acid-alkaline balance in all the body tissues, but most importantly in the bloodstream, the lymphatic system, the mouth, the stomach, the small and large intestines, the urinary tract, the vagina, and portions of the lower bowel. All of these locations carry slightly different levels of pH (hydrogen-ion concentration). Altering that acidity or alkalinity in any significant manner can spell disease. Even minor changes can bring about a state of dis-ease, of feeling not just right—the beginning of an illness. Restful sleep or exercise can make the body more alkaline, while worry makes it more acid.

Food is by far the most important factor in

maintaining an acid-alkaline balance in the human body, depending on the food's acid or alkaline ash content. This was determined years ago. And the acidity or alkalinity manifests itself in the various fluids and tissues of the body, depending on how well balanced the body is in its state of health.

Thus, the food that we eat really gives us food for thought, doesn't it?

The American Cancer Society has a film available to loan entitled *The Embattled Cell*. Part of the research it portrays is the manner in which lymphocytes (white blood cells) move through the tissues of the body, attacking cancer cells and killing them. It also shows lymphocytes that have obviously been done in by the cancer cells. A war is constantly going on inside the body between the invaders and the defenders of the body.

It stretched our minds to realize that the awareness of the lymphocytes—as they sought out and destroyed the cancer cells—implied that *all* of the cells of our body must have their own type of consciousness, their own job to do in the physiology of the body.

Lymphocytes function normally in the slightly alkaline medium of the lymphatic stream. When the lymph becomes more acid, the lymphocytes cannot function normally. Thus they are liable to lose the battle. Much can be theorized about the effect of the acid-alkaline balance in the body regarding health and disease, but it has not been thoroughly researched, so there is no proof. A person does not need scientific proof, however, when good diet works astonishing changes in his or her own body.

As we studied what Edgar Cayce said about diet, we developed what we called a "Basic Diet"—one that will keep a person well adjusted as far as food is concerned. This is included later in the book.

As the years gave us more experience and as we worked with the concepts of physiology found in the Cayce material, we adopted what might be called a *physiological* approach to therapy. We found that the physiology of the body can be altered to move it toward more normal functioning.

It led us into a multilevel approach to diagnosis and treatment. We began to understand that poor absorption of foods in the upper intestinal tract does not stand by itself as a syndrome. Rather, other so-called "diseases" can arise as a result of the deficiency in food substances created by the malabsorption. The blood-forming organs may cease to function up to par, for instance, and the individual becomes anemic. A variety of secondary problems can arise from a lack of proper absorption or assimilation. To correct such conditions may require treatment of the intestinal tract, improvement of the diet, restoration of a better acid-alkaline balance, and changes in attitudes and emotional patterns—in short, the adoption of a new, more health-producing life-style.

Assimilation is the process that takes food through a multitude of steps. It begins with its entry into the mouth and its breakdown with the enzymes in the saliva. Then the food goes through the stomach and small intestine, where it is acted upon by the acids and enzymes and bile so that it is finally absorbed by the lining of the intestinal tract into the capillaries or the lymphatc stream.

Finally it is taken by the lymphatics into the bloodstream, or more directly by the hepatic circulation through the liver, where it might undergo further change in preparation for utilization by the cells of the body where rebuilding of tissue can come about. All of the steps are necessary in this enlivening of the human body is called *assimilation.*

Then, when cells die in the metabolic process going on within the body, these remnants must be *eliminated* through the four eliminatory channels of the body—the liver/intestinal tract, the kidneys, the lungs, and the skin. Keeping the assimilation and the elimination proper and balanced helps tremendously in maintaining health. Cayce said it in one reading like this:

> . . . would the assimilations and the eliminations be kept in nearer *normal* in the human family, the days might be extended to whatever period as . . . desired.

> 311–4

But one great concept empowered me in my growing understanding of the body: the idea that the human body, if encouraged to return back to normal, will inevitably overcome any illness, *if* the right kind of aid is available and the patient is willing to continue applying those aids patiently, persistently, and consistently. The aids *always* include dietary adjustments and corrections. They nearly always include the use of the mind in changing attitudes and emotional patterns. But the goal is possible, if the directions are followed.

The first years of my practice expanded my

medical school training into a variety of concepts—a horizontal kind of reaching out with my mind. In more recent years, Edgar Cayce has brought me into an understanding of the body—an in-depth vertical, spiritual study, which adds richness to exploring why we need to pay attention to the food we eat.

Much of what has been discussed here will be dealt with more extensively later on in the book, as we move first to an understanding of what commonsense eating really is.

2

※

COMMONSENSE DIET—
WHAT IS IT?

MANY DIETS—MANY VALUES

This book came into being not because I really wanted to write about diet—in medical school we were never taught about foods, diets, or nutrition, except that dieticians were trained to teach our patients about how they should eat. The book really came about because I recognized the common sense inherent in the Edgar Cayce readings— and because I felt the importance of sharing what I had realized of that quality, as it relates to what we feed our physical bodies during this time we spend on the Earth.

A commonsense approach might be typified by the current bit of wisdom that says, "If it works, don't fix it." It's not what you would call a scientific approach. Rather, it is an attitude toward something that says, "This is obvious! Let's go ahead."

Several years ago, a physician lectured about nutrition at the American Holistic Medical Association's annual meeting. He was of the opinion that there were as many diets now available as there were physicians and self-appointed nutritionists.

Physicians do offer diets to their patients to treat this or that disease, and the medical profession has now grudgingly agreed that certain diets protect the human being from colon cancer and heart disease. People follow diets to lose weight, to gain weight, to stay healthy, and to improve their bodies, especially if they have fallen ill.

We probably don't think of it often, but *all* of us are on a diet of one sort or another, whether we realize it or not. Most often, the diet is imposed on us by our appetites, not through the conscious action of choosing to eat in a certain way.

In looking at the field of nutrition and diets, common sense would dictate that we not give the same diet to a six-month infant that we offer a grown man. Nor would we expect a 220-pound man to eat the same diet that his 105-pound wife would need for maintaining health. We may know, for instance, that chocolate is not good for a clear complexion, but we *like* chocolate and so we eat it. Our unconscious wins out over our conscious knowledge because of patterns we call appetites.

Common sense, in the light of the Edgar Cayce material, not only takes these obvious facts into consideration, but expands the picture by painting humankind in a different hue. Each of us, according to this body of information, is a spiritual being first and foremost. Each was created in the image of God, as a soul, made up of spirit, mind, and will. Then we came into the Earth dimension as body, mind, and spirit, on an adventure to find our way back to where we started.

All of us have been here over and over, one lifetime after another, gaining spiritually in one life, losing in another. Within each of us, then, has been built a memory bank of information, habits, attitudes, and beliefs that indeed makes each of us unique among all the billions of individuals on the Earth.

It makes sense, then, that our appetites would be our own, that our attitudes toward what we *think* would be a good diet also would be unique. In our unconscious minds each of us has built appetites from eating, over and over again, foods that we like. These then become habits that we call appetites. The foods we like are not necessarily the foods that would be best for us. We know that to be true in all of our experiences. So we need to find out what is constructive for our bodies, and we must develop habits of liking that rather than being obedient to habit patterns from the unconscious mind.

That's the kind of common sense to be found in the Cayce readings. And my own experience working with these concepts at the level of the practice of medicine says that this is the common sense I find practical and usable. In one reading, Cayce had this to say:

First—the physical body is the temple, the encasement of the mind and soul of the entity. It has its virtues, its faults, its weaknesses, its strengths. Yet, as is understood, he that is wholly—mentally, spiritually—in accord with the oneness of the Christ-Consciousness may expect and may live and may know within self the PROPER course for the activities to bring the best welfare for the body . . .

Thus, not such a diet as to be contrary to natural laws, but that which is in keeping with the manner in which the body exerts self—so that there may be brought the better resuscitating influences and forces.

1662–1

In using the Cayce readings for creating a commonsense diet, it is important to realize that Cayce (in his physical readings) communicated directly with the unconscious mind of another individual and collected his information while he was in an altered state—much like the disciple John experienced when he wrote the book of The Revelation. Cayce did this almost nine thousand times, always making contact with the person seeking help.

In making that contact, Cayce apparently found that the food that would be best for an individual was that which would influence the physiology of the body in a manner that was most constructive. And it was always in accord with that person's physical-mental-spiritual makeup. Cayce's recommended diet was also determined by the kind of illness or dis-ease, or physiological imbalance that was to be found in the individual's body.

Cayce did not see illness as a true reality. Rather, he saw the human being as an entity in

time and space, with illnesses coming about because of lessons the individual needed to learn. Or
because of failing to obey the laws of function of
the human body or perhaps the laws of the universe itself. Or of the mind. Or even of the spirit.

Thus, the suggestions about diet depended
most definitively upon the person for whom the
reading was given, rather than upon the problem
facing the individual at the time. The problem was
secondary. Even the diet was not of prime importance. The human being was always accorded first
priority. There are numerous instances of how
this kind of a concept might be illustrated. This is
one:

Q-5: Should I have a special kind of diet?
A-5: As indicated, a generally well balanced diet,
adhering to the warnings indicated in order to
keep a balance, stressing certain characters of
foods. But do not become so diet-conscious as for
the diet to become master, rather than the self
being master of the diet.

2454-1

It is important to recognize that a disease process
is often associated with or caused by certain dietary habits (where the diet became master) that
may be deeply ingrained in a person's consciousness. Diabetes in the adult male or female is one
example of this, where poor diet habits essentially
cause the diabetes, and the laws of the body have
consciously or inadvertently been broken. Then
comes the result: a disease. There are other particular problems associated with eating habits. But
no human being is without relationship to the

effect of his or her diet on the health and general welfare of the body. Cayce suggested that you can choose the diet desired rather than letting the appetite habits of your body rule:

> . . . though never get the body in that position wherein the body does not control the appetite rather than appetite controlling [the] system ∴ . .
>
> 106–7

In looking at the information in the Cayce readings, then, toward creating a nutritional program, you must take each reading as a unit, as a recommendation for that person for whom the reading was given. Out of such a search can come certain rules, suggestions, and principles to which you can apply yourself and gain out of it the makings of a reasonable and truly commonsense diet. Because, if you are honest with yourself, it will work for you.

HINTS ABOUT A COMMONSENSE DIET

Here are a few general hints that will get you started on thinking about and creating your own constructive, commonsense eating habits, which we generally call a diet. I'll elaborate on most of these in later chapters in the book.

About What You Are

> . . . Realize that each soul is as the temple of the living God, even as thy own body. Thus be mindful more not of the body for body's sake, but of the body that the tem-

ple of the living God may be the better
channel for the manifesting of the spiritual truths. . . .

2938-1

About Salads

Have at least one meal each day that includes a quantity of raw vegetables; such
as cabbage, lettuce, celery, carrots, onions and the like. Tomatoes may be used
in their season.

2602-1

About the Evening Meal

Evenings—preferably this would be the
heavier or the more varied meal. In meats,
if these are taken, we would use only fish,
fowl, or lamb. No fried foods ever at any
time. Have more leafy vegetables, rather
than those of pod or the root nature or
those that grow under the ground.

1567-1

About Water

. . . Well to drink *always plenty* of water,
before meals and after meals—for, as has
oft been given, when any food value *enters*
the stomach *immediately* the stomach
becomes a storehouse, or a medicine
chest that may create all the elements
necessary for proper digestion within the
system. If this *first* is acted upon by
aqua pura, the reactions are more near
normal . . .

311-4

About Attitudes

Keep in that of constructive thought; because, to be sure, the thoughts of the body act upon the emotions as well as the assimilating forces. Poisons are accumulated or produced by anger or by resentment or animosity. Keep sweet!

23–3

About Acid-Alkaline Balance

. . . For in all bodies, the less activities, there are in physical exercise or manual activity, the greater should be the amount of alkaline-reacting foods taken. *Energies* or activities may burn acids, but those who lead the sedentary life or the non-active life can't go on sweets or too much starches—but these should be well-balanced.

798–1

About Foods Grown Locally

As indicated, use more of the products of the soil that are grown in the immediate vicinity. These are better for the body than any specific set of fruits, vegetables, grasses, or what not. . . .

4047–1

About Combinations to Avoid (In Brief)

Starches and sweets at the same meal—too much acidity.

Several starchy foods together—too much acidity.

Meat and potatoes—or meat and bread—or meat and starch upsets digestion.

Citrus fruits and cereals at the same meal—creates drosses.

Coffee or tea taken with milk or cream—hard on digestion.

About Foods to Avoid

Fried Foods.

Carbonated drinks, generally.

White sugar, white flour products.

Red meats or heavy meats not well cooked.

Pork products—except bacon cooked very crisp.

3

※

YOUR BODY IN HEALTH
AND DISEASE

A TRUE STORY

Cancer of the rectum is not a pleasant thing to discover in your body. Left unattended, it can, of course, destroy the body. Surgery is the most obvious approach to correcting the problem, and seventeen years ago, when Isabelle was diagnosed as having a rectal cancer, the therapy proposed was an abdominal-perineal resection. This means that the entire rectum and part of the colon would be removed and a colostomy would be created on the abdominal wall.

Isabelle, in her mid-fifties, was a registered nurse and knew what all this meant—and she didn't want surgery. She was well informed about the Edgar Cayce material and wanted to undergo a treatment that was in tune with his suggestions. She chose a therapy program at the A.R.E. Clinic that extended over a period of nearly eighteen months. When the program was completed, her surgeon removed the shrunken bit of tissue locally—what was left of the cancer—and her body was whole again. In seventeen years, no sign of cancer has recurred.

The therapy program included therapeutic massages, colonics, violet ray treatments, counseling, biofeedback, and regular medical evaluation, but the one thing I recall most vividly was the diet. In the Cayce readings on cancer, one suggestion was to eat fresh green leafy vegetables such as a cow or a rabbit would eat. This is certainly sufficient for both the cow and the rabbit, but human beings are not constituted to find such a diet very palatable, filling, or satisfying.

Isabelle followed such a diet, however, eating nothing but green salads for nearly nine months. She lost about twenty pounds during the first couple of months, then stabilized and stayed at a constant weight. Later on, fruit was gradually added to her diet until the surgeon pronounced her cured. What brought the cure? Mainly the diet, but the various therapies, her attitudes of constructive belief, and the prayers others offered all contributed their part.

Our bodies are surely tremendous creations. I think the following reading would have pretty well covered Isabelle's state of health and identified the various physiological changes that were occurring in her body, although the reading itself was given for someone else, years earlier:

. . . But we would make changes in the manner in which the assimilations are carried on, the manner in which the circulations are distributed through the impulses from various ganglia or centers along the cerebrospinal system from which organs of the body may be made to properly coordinate; the organs of the pelvis as well as the hepatic circulation and the activities to the respiratory system.

Thus there may be allowed the elimination of drosses, the elimination of energies or used forces that become as drosses in the activity of the system; so that the activity may become nominal or normal. . . .

1073–1, p. 2

Getting rid of a cancer is not simply removal of the group of cells that are apparently causing the difficulty. It means correcting the basic cause of the problem—whether it be attitudes, circulation, neurology, acid-alkaline balance, or whatever—and changing the physiology of the body so that it functions constructively, not in a destructive manner to bring death to the body. This is the manner in which Cayce saw the "forces" within the body acting, always related to emotions, stresses, attitudes, and the belief patterns of the unconscious mind.

THE NATURE OF YOUR BODY

From the point at which conception occurs until the human being is a grown adult, there is a pattern the body fulfills that is called a genetic pattern, but which is as yet not really understood.

25

For the purposes of this book, we will explore Edgar Cayce's interpretation of genetic patterns, for this man, in his unconscious state, apparently tapped universal sources of information.

The very first thing that occurs in conception is that the sperm and the egg join forces. A globular nucleus is formed, which is the beginning of the pineal gland. From that beginning, there is a kind of a force field created, or—as Cayce called it—an aerial, which extends from the nucleus and creates the central area from which the rest of the body gradually develops.

The external, timeless body is really an energy complex of a finer vibration around which the atoms of this dimension are congregated to form you or me.

The fully formed body, then, is a structure of energy. For what is an atom, really, but potential energy? The body is a manifestation of duality, since each atom has positive and negative charges. And the body is primarily an electrical creation, with each movement, each breath becoming an electrical manifestation through the nervous system and the various tissues of the body.

In a number of the readings, Cayce suggested that electricity was, in the earth, a manifestation of God, or Creative Forces—*not* God, but the *manifestation* of God:

> . . . Know then that the Force in nature
> that is called electrical or electricity is that
> same force ye worship as Creative or God
> in action . . .

1299-1

26

. . . whatever electricity is to man, that's what the power of God is. Man may in the material world use God-Force, God-Power or electricity, to do man's work or to destroy man himself. . . .

3618–1

If this is true, while those forces of Creation are moving through us, the various parts of ourselves are conscious of that movement, at least to some degree. For the cells of our bodies—even the atoms comprising those cells—have their own type of consciousness.

Each one of us is really, then, in a relationship with universal forces and with every atom of our bodies. Through the Forces of Creation, we are also in touch, at some level, with all people throughout the earth—and probably with those in other dimensions, too.

The parts of our bodies, then, that bring us life—the internal organs and systems that can well be called the life support systems—all have their own degree of consciousness and must work cooperatively and in coordination with each other, in order that perfect health should come about.

That means that the organs of elimination—the lungs, the kidneys, the skin, and the liver/intestinal tract—must be coordinated in their activity. The lungs and the upper intestinal tract are part of the assimilatory system, and *they* must also coordinate their activities.

The internal secreting glands (the endocrines) also affect each other through their nervous system attachments, their hormones placed into the bloodstream, and, undoubtedly, through their own areas of consciousness, much as it is with the other organs and systems.

It is extremely fortunate for us, in our present state of development, that all of these things work fairly well, even if they are only given half an opportunity to do so, for it would be difficult to live a normal life if we had to direct the beating of the heart with our conscious minds. Think of it a moment, and you will appreciate the manner in which this wonderful body of ours works to keep us alive and healthy. We do indeed need to cooperate with the efforts that are found within.

The lymphatic system, under the direction of the thymus gland, one of the endocrine organs, is our protective system. If it is up to par at any given time, for instance, you will not be subject to catching a cold or acquiring any infection. This is the immune system, the force within our bodies that will try to reject an organ transplant, because the new organ is foreign to the body. The immune system keeps out all foreign invaders, if it is doing its job properly.

Our lymphatics naturally do become depressed at times, mostly because of stresses, but often because of what we have been feeding our bodies. The diet, then, plays an important part in our health. Because every part of the body has a pH—that is, an acidity or an alkalinity, a hydrogen-ion concentration—it is important to keep the body in its normal acid-alkaline balance. This is probably no easier to accomplish constantly than it is to keep harmony all the time in a family of ten or twelve children, for all parts of the body have their own electrical and acid-alkaline nature and their own consciousness.

When food is metabolized it creates within the functioning parts of the life support system a reaction that is acid or alkaline—or, we might say, a specific pH (hydrogen-ion concentration) that is either high (alkaline) or low (acid).

Cayce saw foods having their effect on portions of the body because of their acid-alkaline balance or because the foods did not combine well within the body and caused drosses or acids or poisons in the body. Thus his comments about the proper diet were to a large extent associated with these two qualities—the acid-alkaline balance, and food combinations. The following readings exemplify the manner in which he treats these questions:

Q-5: Any advice regarding the diet?
A-5: As indicated, keep to those that are more alkaline than acid. Those that are naturally easily assimilated, and that make for increase in the lymph and the blood flow. . . .

642–1

The conditions then to be met are those about the portion where the lesion exists, and the effect same has upon the system—especially producing the fermentation, or acidity *and* fermentation, in an improper proportion and manner.

There has been taken recently properties that have started the secretions from the liver. This adding to the system under the existent conditions, produces

29

or causes the extra or *over* amount or condition of acidity.

. . . The lower portion of the intestinal system should be kept, then, nearer in the state of non-acidity, or alkaline. Keep those food values, those medicinal properties, that tend to produce for the system a nearer equalized condition in this respect. Foods entering should be *alkaline* in reaction. When acted upon by gastric juices they become acid, but should be alkaline reaction in the lower digestion.

294–113

Vegetables and fruits, with few exceptions, are alkaline-reacting, while meats, starches, and sugars are generally acid-reacting.

And, for a fifty-one-year-old woman who was having problems with dermatitis, obesity, and pelvic disorders, Cayce had this to say about combinations in dietary practices:

. . . As to the matter of the diets, these become naturally—with the general conditions of the body—a necessary element or influence. Do not ever take cereals *and* grapefruit or citrus fruits or pineapple juices *at* the same meal. Have the cereal one day and the fruit the next; *never* the two at the same meal. For they form in the system, together, that which is not beneficial—and *especially* not helpful for this body, forming an acid that fattens the body. Coffee or tea should preferably be

30

without milk or cream, for again we find that the combination of the acids—or the tannic forces, the chickory, or the properties that are the food values to the digestive forces—becomes disturbing, when combined outside of the body. However, if milk and coffee are taken at the same meal—but not combined before they are taken—the gastric juices flowing from even the salivary glands in the mouth so taking these *change* the activity so that the food values of both are taken by the system, in the activity through the alimentary canal. . . .

. . . Wines, or such natures, may be taken more preferably *as* food; not as those that would be taken *with* food. Hence red wine—that is, Sherry or Port, or such natures—taken with sour bread, or black bread, in the late afternoon—rather than coffee or tea—is much more preferable; and it doesn't put on weight, it doesn't make for souring in the stomach—if taken in that manner; but not with other foods! . . .

1073–1

DEFENDING THE BODY WITH FOOD

In the eighties a new specialty was born in the field of medicine called psychoneuroimmunology—the study and application of the information linking the mind, the nervous system, and the immune system together. For it is well understood in this field that the mind and all that encompasses the mind, attitudes, and emotions work directly or indirectly with the thymus system (the lymphatic/immune system) to either aid or harass the body and its ability to stay healthy—or to overcome a disease process.

The nervous system is always intricately involved in this procedure, for it registers input through the senses that "make" one angry or sad, happy or fearful, according to the habit patterns of emotion that have been stored up, as in a computer, within the unconscious mind of the perceiver.

It is understood in physiology that the lymphatic stream is normally alkaline. Thus, the defenses of the body are usually up to par when the immune system is balanced in regard to the acid-alkaline ratio within the body. It is then that the lymphocytes, monocytes, and neutrophils are at their best in fighting off invaders—and in rebuilding the body.

Foods play a key role in protecting the body from illness, in that they can either aid in rebuilding the body, or they can create acids, drosses, and poisons as they enter the body, thus creating more of a problem than solving the existing difficulty.

In researching the Cayce readings, one comes to the same conclusion, however, that is reached in practicing medicine or simply living life: All problems cannot be solved with food or by special diets. In the same manner, a positive frame of mind—positive thinking—cannot be a cure-all.

In my own discipline, the field of medicine, it

has long been the approach to illness that not much really can be done until the diagnosis is made. Then the proper medication can be given and the individual can be healed. Next to nothing is said currently in our medical schools about how attitudes and emotional problems, poor diet practices and long-standing belief patterns, along with life-styles and environmental difficulties really form the basic causative factors for most diseases. These realities must be addressed more definitively in order to gain what might be called true healing of the human body.

No matter what the cause of a problem or what the training of a therapist might be, there is always aid that can be brought to the healing process by the adoption of a properly designed diet. The diet, then, becomes the first line of defense.

How do we use diet, then, as an aid?

Most importantly, according to the information in the Cayce readings, one should avoid poor combinations of foods and then adopt a proper balance of 80 percent alkaline to 20 percent acid content in the foods. These will be dealt with more specifically in Chapter 5.

From the readings, the understanding of *why* these two factors are so important can only be gleaned in bits and pieces. Cayce never gave a discourse on the subject, but he told a little here, a little there—and the picture starts to unfold.

The next selections help us out in this regard, for they seem to indicate that proper conditions of acidity or alkalinity existing in the small intestine and the proper food combinations have a great deal to do with the first steps in assimilating of foodstuffs. And those foods, broken down properly, then need to be carried through the blood and lymph vessels to reach all those areas where rebuilding of cells comes about. This is happening all the time in our bodies—it becomes the essence of regeneration of all the tissues of our bodies:

Q-5: What would be the most appropriate vegetables or foods to build up my blood supply so as to maintain the same pressure throughout?
A-5: As indicated, those that make for the keeping of a normal balance in the acids and alkalines of the system.

Study just a bit the vegetables and the general food values of ALL foods; as to how they react to the body . . . for we would find at times there are various conditions and various foods that produce, under the stress and strain of activity, a varied effect . . .

. . . When the body is under stress or strain by being tired, overactive, and then would eat heavy foods—as cabbage boiled with meat—these would produce acidity; yet cabbage WITHOUT the meats would produce an alkaline reaction UNDER the same conditions! The same would be true if there were fried foods, such as fried potatoes, eaten when there is a little cold or the body has gotten exceedingly cold or damp, these would produce (if fried) an acid, and become hard upon the system; while the same token as mashed or as roasted with other foods would react differently. . . .

1411–2

Then, more about the things that go on in the duodenum, and the early passages of food through the digestive tract:

. . . It will be found to be helpful, then, that the diets be not too much starch nor too much of the sweets or a combination of these. Proteins, citrus fruits, those activities that *make* for keeping an *alkalinity* would be well; or about eighty percent of alkaline-reacting foods to twenty percent of the acids. To be sure, ordinarily proteins are considered acid-reacting. But the *activities* of proteins in the system, when not taken with starch, bring the necessity of the hydrochloric activity in their digestive forces. So when proteins such as from fish, fowl, or lamb are taken, their final reaction through the lower portions of the duodenum becomes nearer to a normal balance of alkalinity. For alkalinity begins with the glands themselves of the mouth. Then with the entrance to the stomach we have a combination of lacteals and hydrochlorics, dependent—of course —upon the nature of the foods or *more* so the *combinations* of same.

So, then, for this particular body, light wines or champagne or those of that nature would be helpful to add a bit of an alcoholic content with the food; that there may be kept those tendencies for a better elimination, a better coordination through those activities in the alimentary canal as well as the gastric flows from the pancreas, the liver and the spleen, as well as the activity of the gall duct for the lacteals' assimilation. . . .

920–8

If the body can be given the proper balance and combination of foods needed (we should probably call them "energies" after they have gone through the early steps of digestion and assimilation), then the defense of the body—the immune system—might be built up to act in a manner better meeting its potential. This means protection for the body from most illnesses and aid in overcoming most problems that affect it.

THE ROLE OF DIET IN REGENERATION AND LONGEVITY

Our bodies are much more wonderful than we ordinarily give them credit for being. Our life span, for instance, is not truly limited. No one has ever really died from old age. Rather, the pathologist finds that what appears to be natural causes really ends up being a disease of one sort or another.

Cayce suggested that often an individual has fulfilled his or her purpose this incarnation and desires to move on. This desire is deep within the soul and often does not come through to the conscious mind.

Today, many people are living to be more than a hundred years of age. Gerontologists—those working with the elderly—will venture different opinions as to the age a person might attain. There are thousands of people who are beyond the century mark both in this country and in Russia, where records are kept with a fair degree of accuracy.

In my own experience in family medicine, I've cared for several centenarians over the years.

Regeneration is simply a rebuilding of tissues of the body to their original state. In a sense, it's making things young again, or rejuvenating the body. If you were to be cut with a knife, and the tissues were brought together surgically and sutured, a scar would develop. That may be healing, but it is not regeneration. Regeneration would come about when or if the tissues were cared for in such a way that no scar developed—or that the scar that had developed completely disappeared. A bone that is fractured goes through many stages but finally regenerates most of the time, since one cannot see where the bone was fractured if the fracture is treated properly.

We need to look with new eyes at the questions of longevity and purpose. If regeneration is always theoretically possible—given that the proper conditions are met—then there are few willing to pay the price to live a long, long time. Or is it that when a person's life purpose is met, then it is time to move on and try again another time?

From the readings it is clear that rejuvenation or regeneration is possible, although as Cayce told one group of questioners, ". . . The body may be revivified, rejuvenated. And it is to that end it may, the body, *transcend* the earth and its influence. But not those standing here may reach it yet!" (262–85)

What part does diet play in achieving an active, healthy, long life? Some insights might be gained from several of the extracts taken from the Cayce readings:

> . . . For as the body is the storehouse of all influences and forces from without, it has the abilities for the creation—with the correct firing or fuel for the body—that which is able to sustain—not only sustain but to recuperate and to rebuild, revitalize, regenerate the activities of the body. . . .
>
> 1334–1

> Then, keep that attitude of constructive, creative forces within self. For all healing of every nature must arise within the self. For there is the ability within the physical body to re-create or reproduce itself, as well as the activities for assimilating that from which the re-creation is to be brought about . . .
>
> 1663–1

> Then there is the ENTITY, the soul body— that may find material manifestation or expression in the ability not only of BODILY procreation but of every atom, every organ within itself to REPRODUCE itself, its likeness, through the assimilation of that taken within—either physically OR mentally. . . .
>
> 2402–1

> . . . Know that even at this period in the experience of the body there is that within the body which WILL replenish, if the

body is kept cleansed from the impurities
of poor eliminations. . . .

1464–1

Certainly, with the storehouse within the
body available, and having at hand dietary suggestions for correcting the functions of assimilations
and eliminations, the possibility of regenerating
becomes more real, doesn't it? Only purpose, desire, and one more quality—ego—stand in the way.
Cayce talked about this, too:

> For, the ability of each functioning of the
> body-forces is to reproduce itself, and as
> long as this continues the body keeps not
> only young but active—mentally, spiritu-
> ally, physically—unless it be drugged by
> its own ego.

3042–1

We can always take the first step toward regeneration by applying with patience, persistence,
and consistency the rules governing attitudes in
commonsense eating—which will be discussed in
the next chapter.

4

❊

ATTITUDES IN DIET AND HEALTH

SPIRITUAL CONCEPTS

Throughout the material in the Edgar Cayce readings dealing with healing of the human body, one concept keeps recurring: the idea that attitudes of a constructive, helpful nature come about through prayer and meditation, and living the concepts that arise from these disciplines.

The fruits of the spirit, as described by Paul in the Bible (Galatians 5:22–23)—love, joy, peace, patience, gentleness, etc.—are all constructive when applied in one's own life, as well as in relationship with other people. These attitudes are just as important to the unity and health of body, mind, and spirit as the fruits of the Earth that we choose to eat are to the alkalinity of our bodies—and our subsequent health.

For more than fifty years, my wife's parents were medical missionaries to India. They always had a minimum of food, and lost significant amounts of weight while in India. Then they came back to this country for a year and a half and fattened up on fried chicken, mashed potatoes, and apple pie as they toured the different churches that sponsored them in India.

Yet, each time they sat down to eat, they prayed that God would bless their food—and I know this changed the vibrations of the food itself. They both lived to be nearly ninety years old, and the manner in which they appreciated whatever food they were given, the laughter that surrounded them as they ate, and the way in which they looked at mealtime as a special time of the day—all these certainly helped to extend their years of service in India.

Did you know that, among the professions, members of the clergy enjoy a greater longevity than all the rest? I'm sure the prayers and the meditations that are part of their daily lives contribute generously to that promise of long life.

Mealtime with someone else has always been a special time for me. I've often wondered why until I read about the experience two of the disciples had, immediately after the resurrection of Jesus (Luke 24:13–32). They walked to Emmaus with Him (not recognizing Him in his altered state), discussing recent events and listening to this man expound on the scriptures that told about what was going to happen—and then they sat down with Him to eat. When He broke bread with them, their eyes were opened and they recognized Him— then He vanished. This was a spiritual experience for both of these men, and I think has something to say about why it is that any of us find eating together today such a special experience, if we will let it be that.

Our bodies require food to stay alive. Food permeates our lives in every way. Each day we choose foods we eat and we eat three meals every day. Food seems to be everywhere. If life was indeed created to be eternal, then what we eat becomes a major part of that spiritual adventure. We need to treat it that way. And one of the ways we can do it is by blessing the food first by prayer.

Cayce spent much of his time while unconscious talking about prayer and meditation. Following are selections from some of his comments:

Prayer

. . . prayer is the *making* of one's conscious self more in attune with the spiritual forces that may manifest in a material world . . .

281–13

Prayer is the concerted effort of the physical consciousness to become attuned to the consciousness of the Creator, either collectively or individually. . . .

281–13

. . . For prayer is a supplication not only to the Creative Forces from within but *to* the Creative Forces, *with* the Creative Forces from without . . .

281–27

. . . For thy prayer is as a supplication or a plea to thy superior; yet thy meditation is that thou art meeting on *common* ground!

281-28

Meditation

. . . Meditation, then, is prayer, but is prayer from *within* the *inner* self, and partakes not only of the physical inner man but the soul that is aroused by the spirit of man from within.

281-13

. . . *Meditation* is *emptying* self of all that hinders the creative forces from rising along the natural channels of the physical man to be disseminated through those centers and sources that create the activities of the physical, the mental, the spiritual man; properly done must make one *stronger* mentally, physically . . .

281-13

What IS meditation? . . . It is the attuning of the mental body and the physical body to its spiritual source . . . it is the attuning of thy physical and mental attributes seeking to know the relationships to the Maker. THAT is true meditation.

281-41

. . . They that would know God, would know their own souls, would know how to meditate or to talk with God, must believe that He IS—and that He rewards those who seek to know and to do His biddings.

281-41

Meditation has become more and more a part of the activity of an increasing number of individuals throughout the world. In this country, it has been slower to develop or become common practice until the last few decades. Those in the Far East have practiced meditation for centuries, and some of these exercises have taken hold in this country.

Today, in most churches of the Protestant Christian denominations, there are inroads being made. Time is often now allotted to a "moment of silence," which is often longer than a moment.

In this moment of silence, if extended sufficiently, there comes the raising of an energy up the spine which touches all seven of the spiritual centers in the body, the seven endocrine glands, and creates a movement in all seven that to an extent purifies them, makes of them better instruments of change for the emotions they bring up to the surface. For the glands are part of what we call the unconscious mind.

When meditation is used, the individual needs to send out the energy raised in this manner as a blessing to others. That's where prayer comes into better use. Quiet first, then prayer.

As you meditate, other changes occur. The body functions improve, achieve better alignment with each other, and systems coordinate and cooperate with each other. Thus foodstuffs entering the digestive tract can be better utilized. And the body becomes healthier.

Laboratory studies have demonstrated physiological changes that occur with meditation—in the nervous system and also in the state of immunity found in the body. One researcher told me recently how several immune factors in the bloodstream were upgraded when his subjects meditated.

Meditation is defined in the readings as an attunement to that Force which gives us life itself. The life force enters the body at the pineal and descends along the spine, bringing life to all parts of the body. The effect of meditation is to raise that life energy which the Creator placed in our bodies along the channels that touch those endocrine centers. And it appears that the two energies are there side by side for us to recognize and communicate with in the process of attunement or at-onement.

Those who have studied this subject in-depth as it is described in the readings say that *every* person must sooner or later learn and practice meditation regularly—it is part of the meditation-prayer combination that leads us back to our Source, which is also our Destiny.

ATTITUDES TOWARD FOOD

So, what do we do about attitudes? There are attitudes, without question, that we should adhere to if we are going to gain the most out of our food to serve the body. Then, too, there are those that we should not exercise or develop but instead gradually let fall by the wayside if we are going to benefit.

It has been said that one should eat to live, *not* live to eat. The difference is great. One uses food to fulfill a life purpose; the other uses life to fulfill an appetite or a group of appetites that are self-satisfying. The great majority of us fall somewhere in-between these two extremes, and I hope trying to eat to live.

If we try using food to benefit our bodies, then the attitudes that are constructive will gradually become more evident and active in our lives, and our bodies, minds, and spiritual purpose in life all will benefit.

We need to know, however, what sorts of attitudes are *not* helpful, *not* constructive in nature, especially as these attitudes relate to food and its use in the body. The negative influences can be as numerous as the positive ones.

First, don't be pessimistic!

> . . . Let the mental attitude also be: *See* those things being accomplished! Not so much of a pessimistic attitude! . . .
>
> 295-4

Second, never eat when you are upset—and this means for any reason. You may have been angry at your husband for being late for dinner. Not good for eating! You may be overtired and exhausted. Wait a while before eating. You may be excited about your first date. Skip the meal. Look to the state of your emotions to determine when you are going to eat. Cayce put my paragraph into just a few words:

> . . . never, under strain, when very tired, very excited, very mad, should the body take foods in the system, see? . . .
>
> 137-30

Third, don't say "I can't eat this" or "I can't eat that." This kind of attitude presupposes that one has sat in judgment, in a sense, on a certain food. For the normal body, all foods may be eaten and enjoyed, although it may take time to retrain the body in understanding what the mind says about this certain situation. But start the process. It will help your body take in the foods that the body may very specifically need. Become friendly to the world of foods that this Earth has provided for you. Cayce also talked about this kind of an attitude:

> . . . As we find, keep this as the rule—rather than studying the diet in such minutia that the body becomes one that can't eat this, or can't eat that, or can't eat the other! Or this would hurt, or that would hurt, or the other would hurt! Because such an attitude becomes as chronic as a disturbing diet! . . .
>
> 1601–1

And, in another way of looking at perhaps the same attitude, it would be well to avoid any kind of unbalanced manner of looking at your diet. In other words, don't be lopsided in your approach to food. This is also what comes from the readings:

> There has existed in the mind as respecting certain characters of diet, that was held for such a period until other things, other conditions, other meals or foods proved to be of detriment to the body, to the body's own undoing. That's why [it's] called lopsided! An even well *balanced*

condition throughout, *not* being too severe in *any* direction! To say that *any* diet that adds proper forces to the body for blood, muscle and nerve building, is in error, is to cut self off—even as to say "This I may do, this I may *not* do"—See?

255–6

If these are attitudes that should be avoided, then what are some of the mental patterns that are helpful building a better body through food? The following reading is rather extensive, but it deals with a very important aspect of eating that says to us, *What purpose, really, do you have in mind when you think about food—what role does food play in your thoughts about your destiny or your purpose this lifetime?*

That thou eatest, see it doing that thou would have it do. Now there is often considered as to why do those of either the vegetable, mineral, or combination compounds, have different effects under different conditions? It is the consciousness of the individual body! Give one a dose of clear water, with the impression that it will act as salts—how often will it act in that manner?

Just as the impressions to the whole of the organism, for each cell of the bloodstream, each corpuscle, is a whole universe in itself. Do not eat like a canary and expect to do manual labor. Do not eat like a rail splitter and expect to do the work of

a mind reader or a university professor,
but be consistent with those things that
make for—even as the universe is builded
. . . One that fills the mind, the very being,
with an expectancy of God will see His
movement, His manifestation, in the
wind, the sun, the earth, the flowers, the
inhabitant of the earth; and so as is
builded in the body, is it to gratify just an
appetite, or is it taken to fulfill an office
that will the better make, the better magnify, that the body, the mind, the soul,
has chosen to stand for? And it will not
matter so much what, where, or when—
but knowing that it is consistent with
that—that is desired to be accomplished
through that body!

As has been given of old, when the
children of Israel stood with the [Dan.
1:5–8] sons of the heathen and all ate
from the king's table, that which was
taken that only exercised the imagination
of the body in physical desires—as strong
drink, strong meats, condiments that
magnify desires with the body—this
builded as Daniel well understood, not for
God's service—but he chose rather that
the everyday, the common things would
be given, that the bodies, the minds,
might be a more perfect channel for the
manifestations of God; for the forces of
the Creator are in every force that is made
manifest in the earth.

341–31

49

We're in the process of choosing ever more perfectly our direction, our purpose—and the foods we use, the functions they perform in the body, are part of that choice!

So, what are some of the other attitudes that should be nurtured in our consciousness, in our minds, in our activities, as we continue to learn more about our bodies and our foodstuffs?

First, let's think of pleasant things. It's so very easy to look at all that is going wrong in the world around us (and, certainly, in the world inside us). But we need to magnify and build on those events, those aspects of peoples' characters that are beautiful; the beauty of the world around us; the wonders that the future holds for us. All these things can build within us a greater coordination between organs that have so much to do with how we use foods. Here are some additional thoughts on the same subject:

> . . . Keep the body—or keep the *mind,* and it will keep the body!—in a constructive manner. That is, think the pleasant things, even when may be the darkest outlook. Do not allow the little things that are hindrances make for irritating, or to hurt the feelings. For naturally the body is sensitive to feelings of others, through the overflow of those activities in the sympathetic system. But know that God IS! Know that He protects those who put their trust in Him; that what is necessary will be supplied thee if ye will keep joyous, keep happy, keep *in* that way of *constructive* forces throughout! 978–1

Second, let's be optimistic. I remember one of the statements in the Cayce material (5325–1) that said, "Expect much, you obtain much. Expect little, you obtain little. Expect nothing, you obtain nothing!" So, what do we expect? It doesn't really cost anything to expect a lot, and if we are clear in that expectation, it will come about. That's the way the universe is put together—our minds have a great deal more to do with what happens, even if we only *think* it and don't *say* it, than most of us will even dream is possible. Another way of saying the same thing:

> Then, the attitude of the body should be kept in that direction of using the abilities in optimistic and creative thought or activity.
>
> 3195–1

Third, try to be patient! I remember another concept I gained from my thirty years of studying these readings: "The try is held to Him for righteousness!" This idea suited me perfectly. I *wanted* to be what might in the better sense be considered righteous, but I knew within my bones that I didn't really qualify, according to the standards I had heard about all my life. When I came across this quote, things changed. I knew I was trying to keep the right attitudes and go in the right direction. This meant that I didn't really need to be 100% all the time—merely that I needed to keep on trying. Failing, sure, at times, but "The try is held to Him for righteousness!"

What the try (and being consistent at it) means is that we need to be patient in order to see the results. Cayce talked often about this kind of human difficulty. This is just one of his discourses on the subject:

Q-4: Approximately how long will it take?
A-4: How long is it until tomorrow, or how long will it take for anything? It depends upon the attitude of the body and the response to the applications. It may be a week, it may be a month, it may be six months or it may be a year! Such depends upon other conditions. . . .

538–70

Obviously, after having had seventy readings from the sleeping Cayce, the woman in this case still had not understood the nature of that quality of the soul we call patience. Nor the real power of the mind. Lots of us would join her in that respect.

Fourth, be constructive about yourself. Don't sell yourself short. Understand your real spiritual nature—that God created you in His image, with His potential that you have not yet unlocked, and you are in the process of unfolding that energy, that power. When you say things about yourself that are derogatory or undermining of your spiritual heritage, you build walls around your true self that are difficult to tear down. Cayce had advice for one who tended to do this:

Q-9: Any other advice?
A-9: These we would do, as we find; and KEEP the spiritual constructive forces AS the attitudes. For if there is ever a condemning of self, it works hardships between the mental and spiritual; and

naturally, for such a sensitive body or entity, works hardships upon the physical.

KNOW—HE is thy strength, thy purpose, thy life!

877–28

And another reading, also dealing with constructive thought, but also the need for patience, persistence, and consistency.

Q-2: Any spiritual advice?
A-2: Keep the mind active in constructive thinking, knowing that what has been the lot, or as the activities, may be used for construction in the whole of the attitude toward Creative Energies. For, all healing must come from that within that is of a spiritual import. Leave the results with the Giver of all good and perfect gifts. Be consistent and persistent in thy physical and thy spiritual and thy mental reactions for the better result. For the laws of the Lord are perfect, converting the soul. And as *He* gained the greater concept of man's position in relation to the world by entering into the flesh and suffering through same, know He, thy Lord, thy Master knows and will aid thee in bearing thy material, thy physical burdens. *Blessed* be His name!

1199–2

Fifth, listen to your inner guidance about what food is best for you. Practice sensing what you need at the present time. Earlier, one of the readings suggested that we not let the diet rule our lives—nor should be make it such a rote kind of a thing that we do not listen to our bodies. Be

53

creative, but be sensitive about your creativity. In other words, there are times when it just doesn't seem right to eat what is in your usual diet. Then, be creative! Don't be rigid. Remember that you are eating to live—and that more abundantly! Not living to eat. Nor are you being a slave to your diet or slave to a diet someone else has recommended. Realize your potential, and know that your inner wisdom can guide you when you call upon it. One woman who obtained a reading got that kind of advice:

Q-3: Are there any suggestions for diet?
A-3: As we find, those that become subject to routine in diet must live by same—and their activities are hemmed. Keep a normal, balanced diet. Of course, as the body has learned, be mindful of not eating heavy meats when under stress or strain. Keep more of an alkaline diet, or those things that make for the better nerve and blood building forces—which will be the *natural* consequences with the properties that we have indicated. As for this body, the better diet would be to eat that the appetite calls for—and whatever it calls for; but don't overload, of course.

696-2

I have a physician friend whom I admire a great deal. His attitude toward food—toward what he puts into his mouth—is exciting. Gladys and I have had him out for dinner and when he sits down at the table and looks at the food, he says, "Wonderful!" And then he proceeds to enjoy and eat every bit of food that comes his way. I suspect it's his attitude that keeps him from gaining weight. But it's exhilarating to eat with him.

One of the Cayce concepts that I have found to be most meaningful in my life—and it applies not only to my general living but also to the food that I eat—states that one should "Magnify the virtues, minimize the faults." If we could do this every time we sit down at the table to eat, our attitudes would truly enhance the manner in which our bodies use the energies that come to us in the form of foods.

NEW HABIT PATTERNS

How do we develop new attitudes toward eating and toward a variety of foods that are not natural to us at the present time? There are many methods presently available to help rid us of old habits and replace these harmful ways of doing things with constructive patterns of activity.

Habits are patterns. They are programmed into our bodies in the same manner as a business plan is programmed into a computer. We are much like a computer—only many would say that a computer is better compared to the human being, but not as magnificent. While the computer always employs a program that has been entered by a capable programmer, the human habit is not quite so simple. You develop a habit by doing something over and over again. For instance, when you start learning how to type, you first have to learn the letters and their placement. Then you must learn where your fingers go. Then the fingers seem to learn their own individual jobs, while your eyes do their part in looking at what you want to type.

Then comes the repetition. Speed goes up from two to three words a minute, when you are really struggling to get started, to where you can begin to brag that you are doing twenty words a minute. If you are really intent, then, on becoming an expert, the speed and accuracy keeps increasing until the desire and the application create—out of your body, your structure, your mind, your desire, and your persistence—an expert typist.

Your ability to be patient with your spouse's annoying habits, no matter how bad they were at the beginning of your marriage, is a habit only when you have exercised it enough that it comes about without your ever thinking of it. It becomes part of *you*! And that's the way you *are*, at that point in time—patient!

You have heard people say, as if in excusing an action they have just created, that "that's just the way I am." They need to begin saying, "This is what I've done with my body and mind, and this attitude is one of my creations." For we have in truth created the manner in which we face life and respond to life's situations, no matter what they may be.

It may be that these emotional responses we've made habitual in our bodies have their origin in the endocrine glands, for Cayce remarked often—and medical science pretty much recognizes this, too—that it is here that memory exists relating especially to emotional patterns.

The adrenal gland, for instance, is known as the "fight-flight gland," bringing the correct physiological responses to emergencies. After the death of a dearly loved one, someone might die of a "broken heart" because the immune system, headed by the thymus gland (the heart center), ceases to function.

We understand that the responses of the endocrine glands instruct the rest of the body to function appropriately to the emotional patterns being awakened which have had their birth somewhere in the past. The endocrines, with their hormonal and neurological connections, orchestrate the responses of every cell, perhaps every atom, of the human body. If the expressions of these patterns are out of harmony with the normal functioning of the physiological forces dealing with the assimilation of foods or the acid-alkaline balance, then disorder in the manner food is utilized by the body will inevitably follow.

The stresses that come to us in our living circumstances bring us great opportunities in creating new habits that are more in line with what we really desire. A stress can be simply trying to get back into your hotel room after you've picked up the morning paper and the door slams behind you and locks—and you are in your undershorts (or slip) without a key. That is stress. Or perhaps another stressful situation is when you feel deflated—as when your boss hands back the story you've written on a special project for the morning edition, with the only comment, "Rewrite it, it lacks punch."

Stress comes to the whole body when you are involved in an argument, especially when it is something you believe in very strongly. There are many kinds of physical stress, but most do not usually involve emotional patterns, unless conflict is involved.

But new habit patterns come about only when

you have the desire to create them. The desire comes when you have chosen an ideal by which to live and then compare your current emotions with what your ideal response might be. At that point dissatisfaction with the current habit patterns arrises and the desire is born to make changes. As you then consciously model your response in accord with your ideal, a new habit then has its beginning and the old one gradually dissipates.

In the Cayce readings, the ideal most often encouraged is that of the Christ. Jesus said, "I am the Way, the Truth and the Light, the Life," and the ideal as identified there means you need to fashion your responses during a time of stress according to the manner in which Jesus did it. Paul called this way of living, the "fruits of the spirit."

When your choices are clarified, the practice of habit making begins. Instead of panicking about being locked out of a hotel room without a room key and dressed minimally, you can be patient enough to simply sit down and read the morning paper or go looking for housekeeping persons. Patience instead of panicking is establishing a new habit.

Habits help—some of them. Other habits hinder. We are in a true sense creatures of habit, so it stands to reason that we need to have the kinds of habits that are helpful, constructive, and worthy of keeping.

Establishing healthy habits requires practice in responding to stresses in a way that is contrary to what we have formed as programs in the past. But the destructive habits, no matter where they may be found, can only be changed by adopting the new in a repetitive manner, practicing the new habit, and making it a part of ourselves. It cannot ever be changed by practicing the old pattern.

Cayce saw the habit as possibly being a boon to the man in the following passage, while recognizing how the wisdom of the body itself can contribute to a better, more normal life as it deals with food and the diet:

Q-7: What foods should the body continue to eat or not to eat?
A-7: These have been outlined again and again. And if the body will just keep such in mind, they may become the HABIT of the body and not that to be dwelt upon; so that the appetites call for those things that are creative and helpful and beneficial, and not have to take thought as to whether "I can eat this today or tomorrow," or as to whether "I have taken this, that or the other, or have left off and not eaten at all" and thus, through the activities produced in the system—which occur at times—those influences are active wherein when the gastric forces attempt to act upon the system they rebel against the very activities and nature of the things taken!

257–202

Attitudes, then, are part and parcel of every human being, sometimes helping in the area of diets and food, and sometimes being hurtful, much as they influence us in life situations throughout our experiences. There is need to bring peace and harmony into the body functions so that good food can then perform good things within—which goes a long way toward rendering the body healthy once again.

Commonsense eating requires setting new goals and ideals about our eating habits and then putting the steps into action that lead toward the goals. We need to eat whole grain products rather than white flour ones—and learn to like them. We need to be joyful instead of argumentative while eating. We need to look at the food in front of us and say, "Wonderful!" rather than being picky about what is served. And we need to teach ourselves constructive habits in selecting healthy foods rather than satisfying ourselves every now and then with a junk food fix.

5

❋

RULES FOR
COMMONSENSE EATING

FOOD IS NOT EVERYTHING

The primary rule in commonsense eating is to recall to your mind over and over again that the Life Force within your own body is always at work influencing your system to bring about a balance in the relationship between your body, your mind, and your spiritual reality.

If you are successful in making close contact with that power (through attitudes, through prayer and meditation, through living the concepts identified with your ideal), then the first step in achieving a coordination within the body functions is accomplished, and you make the move toward health rather than illness or a dis-ease.

Remember that the whole body—physically, mentally, spiritually—is one, and that when the individual parts coordinate even the foods that you choose to use in a diet, there is a better effort within the body to attain a normal balance and activity.

We can understand that the Life Force—the God Force—that gives us life and remains active within our beings is always active, taking what it has at hand, in a sense, and doing the best that it can to create health. Sometimes very strange events can take place.

In Bavaria a number of years ago there lived a woman who led a very unusual life. Theresa Newman became ill with some very difficult physical conditions that were healed through prayer and a dedication to living a life patterned after the life of Jesus. She became a stigmatist, experiencing periodically those wounds that Jesus felt in His crucifixion, and she found that she no longer needed food to live on.

She would go through the stigmata of the cross and would be unconscious for a period of time when she—at one level—felt the pains that Jesus felt. Then, during that time, she would lose pounds of weight from that experience. She needed only to take a consecrated wafer at mass each day, however, and she would work in the fields, never eating more than just that.

Researchers and physicians would check her, even going to the bathroom with her to make sure she had not secreted food away somewhere. She hadn't. Yet she would gain her normal weight back again, until her next stigmatic episode.

Yogananda Paramahansa, in his book *Autobiography of a Yogi* (1981), tells this story with his comment to Theresa that she came to this incarnation with the destiny to show mankind that, as Jesus said, "Man does not live by bread alone."

Few of us have the desire or the need to do

something like what Theresa Newman accomplished. Perhaps the world does not need another similar experience to prove a point. However, insofar as diet is concerned, it does bring sharply to our minds the fact that food is not the primary factor in creating health, nor in bringing about a balance in our whole being. The Life Force does its part as a primary step. Then comes the rest.

One of the readings brings the diet and this principle together for a man who was attempting to build up his body from a rather chronic illness:

Q-4: Is the continued use of anabolic foods recommended?
A-4: This, of course, can be carried to excess; for there is the supplying of elements and the lack of other forces or influences in the anabolic foods that make it rather straining on the body at times. Not too much; or do not depend wholly upon it. For the system always, as Life itself, attempts to use the best it has, to do the best it can with what it has to do with. Hence create a balance in the vitamins and in the amount of the necessary foods for creating a sufficient quantity of heat, but also sufficient quantity of *eliminating* forces—see?

642–1

If we start out our adventure in commonsense eating by recognizing that kind of activity being always present within our bodies, then we need to look at some of the general measures that might be taken to use food creatively and constructively in our bodies.

GENERAL RULES

Perhaps the best way to direct your steps toward what Edgar Cayce might have called commonsense eating would be first to identify those things that need to be learned; second, identify the rules that are best to follow as general measures; and third, identify the "don'ts" that always come into the picture.

Children are most difficult to work with regarding eating patterns, for it seems they invariably *want* those foods that they would do best to avoid: starches, sweets, fried foods, and poor combinations. It helps parents to understand that children can actually get away with more so-called "poor" choices than adults because they burn up energy so rapidly. Just watch a three-year-old in his or her activities, and then try to keep up.

However, that doesn't mean that we should let children eat anything they want. There still are rules of the body.

For adults, however—for those of us who are constantly fashioning our diets by following or disobeying rules of eating that exist, whether we know them or not—there are simple things to be done. Many of these are identified in advice given to individuals in the Cayce material. Others are truly common sense from our own experience. Examples are helpful in understanding how Cayce approached things of this nature:

> . . . Of course, the leafy vegetables are preferable to those that grow under the ground; and of course two or three of the

leafy and one of the pod should be used to one growing under the ground. Lettuce, carrots, celery, and those that may be eaten raw, should be the greater part of one meal every day. . . .

1830-2

. . . Do not have large quantities of any fruits, vegetables, meats, that are not grown in or come to the area where the body is at the time it partakes of such foods. This will be found to be a good rule to be followed by all. This prepares the system to acclimate itself to any given territory.

3542-1

So, what about the simplified general rules of commonsense eating? The first group of rules are those things that must be learned—studied from material later on in this chapter and found in Chapter 7.

1. *Learn* what a well-balanced diet is, and use it.
2. *Learn* which foods are acid-reacting and which ones are alkaline-reacting.
3. *Learn* which foods combine poorly.
4. *Learn* which foods contain which important nutrients and vitamins (see Chapter 7).

Next are the Do's—those rules that need to be put into action rather than avoided. They are the positive factors of choosing the foods, choosing the attitudes, and choosing the habit patterns to be inputted.

1. Bless the food.
2. Let eating with others always be fun. Enjoy the food. Laugh often. "Keep the juices flowing."
3. Use locally grown foods as much as possible.
4. Keep the foods in your diet and on your table as naturally grown as possible. Grow your own if you can.
5. Drink six to eight glasses of water every day. Preferably a glassful before and after each meal, plus two others. Suggestions from the readings say that it is not good to drink water with the meal.
6. Have one meal every day composed of nothing but a fresh green salad. This can be altered with soup on occasion.
7. Have four alkaline-reacting foods to one acid-reacting food in your diet.
8. Have two or three vegetables grown above the ground to one grown below the ground.
9. Keep the assimilations and the eliminations balanced as much as possible.

Next, as a general rule, these following items are the Don'ts in your adventure in commonsense eating.

1. Avoid fad diets. They invariably lead to some difficulty.
2. Avoid poor food combinations (discussed later in this chapter).
3. Avoid overeating.
4. Avoid "bolting" your foods (swallowing without chewing well).

5. Avoid heavy foods at lunchtime.
6. Don't expect the same good diet to meet your needs in every situation or in every condition of health you may experience. Use your common sense.
7. Don't forget to read the ingredient labels and exercise good judgment when shopping for your food.
8. Avoid at all times fried foods, white flour, and white sugar.
9. Avoid pork products and fats, except for crisp bacon.

THE ACID-ALKALINE BALANCE AND FOOD COMBINATIONS

Every food, when it is taken into the body and metabolized, has an effect on the acid-base balance within the body. It may be difficult to measure, but the effect is indisputable.

If an individual were to eat only acid-reacting foods for a period of several days, a change could be noted in the acidity of the sputum and in the urine, or in the pH level of some body fluids or tissues. There are factors that influence the amount of change to be expected, however. One of these is the metabolic level of the body: Does it have a vigorous metabolism, or is the person quiet, retired, and relatively inactive?

Exercise seems to burn up the metabolites of acid-reacting foods, or of those combinations of food that cause an acid reaction. An example is the young teenaged boy who is active in one of the body-contact sports or track, for instance. He could eat citrus fruits and cereal at the same time and get away with it—with no detrimental effects. The same is true of an adult who has a job with strenuous exercise involved in it.

The Cayce readings give great importance to the concept of an acid-alkaline balance in the foods we eat. One of the reasons for this emphasis is that physiologically, imbalances do come about when foods that are improperly combined are taken into the stomach. Another reason is that the body only maintains its state of health and balance when an 80 percent alkaline and 20 percent acid diet is regularly taken.

The body can maintain a homeostasis of sorts for a long period of time under adverse conditions of the diet, but when these poor habits of eating continue, the balance is overturned and an illness results.

How do we know about the pH of a food, for instance? Work has been done in many laboratories to show that when a food is rendered to ash, it does have a specific acidity or hydrogen-ion concentration (pH). To find specific values for a variety of foods, consult the booklet *Preserving Your Alkaline Reserve*. In it, Dr. Arthur Snyder, Ph.D., lists a numerical value for many of the foods you might find in your present diet.

It has been mentioned earlier that the immune system functions best in an alkaline medium. Foods that have an alkaline ash, then, help establish an alkalinity in the immune system whenever most illnesses make their appearance. The diet is not the only factor, of course. Exercise, adequate rest, meditation, laughter, nonstressful situations, massages, autogenic exercises, and certain kinds of packs applied to the body all contribute to body alkalinity that is constructive.

Yet a balance must be kept that is most helpful to the body. This involves not only the alkalinity of the food or its acidity, but also how such foods are combined. The Cayce readings help in understanding what happens in circumstances where poor combinations are used. They also insist repeatedly that there *is* an optimum balance between the acids and alkalines as far as body health is concerned:

> And with the diets, keep these in the eighty percent alkaline to twenty percent acid-producing. Beware of combinations. Keep the acid-producing—or the necessity of the flow of the gastric juices or of acid, which is for certain foods—combined properly. And do not mix starches with sweets. Do not have white bread as a portion of the diet, nor white potatoes. Most other foods in general may be taken.
>
> 1201–1

Q-2: What change may be made in diet, if any?
A-2: As indicated, that to meet the varying surroundings, the climatic reactions; or to make the proper balance of keeping toward the proper alkalinity, is the more preferable. For, as the body ages, there are the tendencies to make for an acidity. The alkalinity, of course, may be overdone. But keep a *general* alkaline-reacting diet. Or, rather let the body follow its desires—with these conditions in mind, that the greater the alkalinity the less chance there is for cold or for congestion.

975–3

In the diets keep close to those that have been indicated. Be cautious of the combinations, rather than the characters of foods, see? Do not have citrus fruits or the acid fruits *with* starches at the same meal. Do not have too much of proteins with the acids, for there is a variation in the character of the reactions in the system; that is, between the hydrochloric and the lacteals. The hydrochloric becomes necessary in proteins, see? As do the alkaline for starches. Yet when these are combined improperly, there is the lack or the excess of one or the other in the system, thus producing an unbalancing and making for excesses in the activities of glandular forces in many ways and manners. Hence these are a portion of the considerations in keeping proper balance in weight, proper balance in activity and in eliminations.

338–5

It is not the intent of this book to clarify or detail the physiology of digestion or assimilation (and elimination), but it can be seen from those things quoted from the Cayce material that he saw the functioning of the body as a major factor in how healthy the body stays and what truly constitutes the best diet in various states of body health.

We need to examine next what constitutes a basic diet, what the acid and alkaline-reacting foods are, what are some poor combinations, along with other factors influencing a basic good diet.

A BASIC DIET OUTLINE

We have used the diet shown in the following chart at the Association for Research and Enlightenment (A.R.E.) Clinic over the past several years for the majority of our patients. It incorporates many of the rules of commonsense eating that we have been talking about. It represents something that nearly anyone can use.

If you are interested in creating your own diet, this might be a good starting point. But you will need to know more about food than is shown in these four circles. You might want to make up your own four circles and create a diet based on your own body needs.

The information in the Cayce readings varied a bit each time a suggested diet was offered. You may feel that the diet chart would be one that is appropriate for you. Remember, you *do* have that knowledge within you that can give you the best guidance about what you need to eat—and that, at the same time, would give you pleasure in accepting.

Q-6: What diet should the body take?
A-6: In the morning, fruit juices, hot or dry cereal, but do not mix them as they will cause acidity. Honey is very good, also cakes such as wheat cakes and buckwheat cakes.

Noon: Green vegetables in the form of salad with those of meat juices and that of broths.

Night: A greater amount of vegetables, and the meats that will aid in the strength of the vitality.

3836–1

71

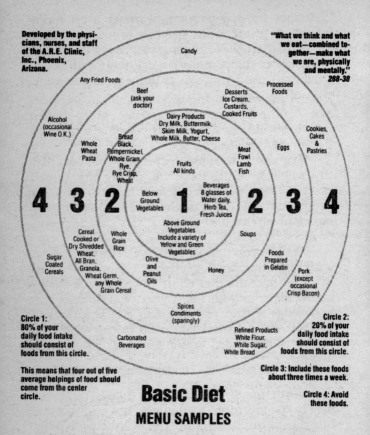

Developed by the physicians, nurses, and staff of the A.R.E. Clinic, Inc., Phoenix, Arizona.

"What we think and what we eat—combined together—make what we are, physically and mentally."
288-38

Candy

Any Fried Foods

Beef (ask your doctor)

Desserts Ice Cream, Custards, Cooked Fruits

Processed Foods

Alcohol (occasional Wine O.K.)

Dairy Products Dry Milk, Buttermilk, Skim Milk, Yogurt, Whole Milk, Butter, Cheese

Cookies, Cakes & Pastries

Whole Wheat Pasta

Bread Black, Pumpernickel, Whole Grain, Rye, Rye Crisp, Wheat

Meat Fowl Lamb Fish

Eggs

Fruits All kinds

4 3 2

Below Ground Vegetables

1

Beverages 8 glasses of Water daily, Herb Tea, Fresh Juices

2 3 4

Above Ground Vegetables Include a variety of Yellow and Green Vegetables

Soups

Cereal Cooked or Dry Shredded Wheat, All Bran, Granola, Wheat Germ, any Whole Grain Cereal

Whole Grain Rice

Olive and Peanut Oils

Honey

Foods Prepared in Gelatin

Sugar Coated Cereals

Pork (except occasional Crisp Bacon)

Spices Condiments (sparingly)

Circle 1: 80% of your daily food intake should consist of foods from this circle.

Carbonated Beverages

Refined Products White Flour, White Sugar, White Bread

Circle 2: 20% of your daily food intake should consist of foods from this circle.

This means that four out of five average helpings of food should come from the center circle.

Circle 3: Include these foods about three times a week.

Basic Diet

MENU SAMPLES

Circle 4: Avoid these foods.

BREAKFAST
Citrus fruit or cereal (do not combine these at the same meal), boiled or scrambled egg, whole wheat toast, glass of milk.

LUNCH
Have a completely RAW lunch and/or vegetable soup. Include green leafy vegetables in a combination salad with oil dressing or mayonnaise, one slice bread and butter, and a beverage.

DINNER
Meat: Fish, fowl, or lamb, cooked vegetables. Include a variety of above and below ground, yellow and green vegetables. Dessert if desired, and a beverage.

It may be that you would prefer a bit more extensive latitude in the specifics of your diet. The following, then, would be more to your liking. But do remember that these were all given for different individuals. And you are an individual with your own unique dietary needs:

As to the diet, this would be an outline; of course, this is not all, but should be the principal portion of the diet:

Mornings—citrus fruit juices combining the orange and lemon juice, grapefruit or pineapple; also a coddled egg using only the yolk of same, Sanka coffee or Ovaltine or the like as a strengthening, with only whole wheat bread well-toasted—and butter may be used with same.

Noons—preferably the juices of vegetables as combined with the juices of meats, and a *well*-balanced vegetable salad made of green vegetables combined with such as celery, lettuce, tomatoes, onions, peppers, radish, carrots, and the like, with which there may be used a salad or an oil dressing.

Evenings—well-cooked vegetables with only meats consisting of fowl or lamb. No fried meats or fried foods of any kind. No potatoes. Preferably leafy vegetables. When there is a bulbular vegetable taken, there should at least be two of the leafy character to counteract it or to balance the meal.

806–1

Cayce seldom gave the same instructions in the identical format. Rather, he varied his bits of information nearly every time. The following group of suggestions might be the kind of menu that would suit your taste best:

In the matter of the diet, it becomes rather necessary that the foods be such as to make for the body-building and the creating of those influences necessary for that as may be assimilated properly in or for the system.

Mornings—we find that citrus fruit juices, raw fruits, or whole wheat, should form the principal part; though these should be altered and not taken at the same meal—that is, do not take the citrus fruits *and* cereals together, you see, or at the same meal. These food values we need in order to keep a normal balance in the acids and the alkalines for the body.

Noons—a portion of the noon meals should preferably consist of raw vegetables; not always, but a portion of same at times. Or shellfish, fish, things that partake of the iodines that are supplied through such; or the phosphorous that comes from such would be most helpful to create a balance in the system (especially if the diathermy and the treatments as indicated are kept).

Evenings—preferably the well-cooked vegetables, and not any *red* meats or any fried foods. And the vegetables should consist of three to four above the ground to one below; that is, in that proportion. Lamb, fowl, wild game—these are preferable for the meats.

1030–1

For different conditions and different people, Cayce, of course, found different approaches to be necessary. The next three offer a menu that might be followed for weakness; then one for building up the blood and the nervous system; then one to stimulate the body:

Q-8: What food should the body eat each meal of the day?
A-8: This would come under the direction rather of dietetics, than of diagnoses of the conditions—for these would vary from time to time. But as the general, this would be an *outline* for a diet for the body:

Morning meals would consist of fruit *juices*, and of cereals.

The lunch meal should consist of soups, or of those broths that are of the strengthening nature.

Those in the evening should consist of vegetables and of little meats. As much green vegetable as is digestible for the body.

Do not add fruits with soups, or do not add fruits or fruit juices with any vegetable forces; for—for the body, and condition—they produce undue fermentation in the body.

Be consistent. Be persistent, see?

325–17

In the diet we would have those things that are body and blood and nerve building. This would be as an outline; not that these are the only things to be taken, but the greater portion:

Mornings—citrus fruit juices; or the small fruits with cereals (such as berries and the like)—and those tending toward the alkaline reacting, and not milk with these but rather the fruit juices, unless only cereals are taken.

Noons—vegetable *juices*, used at the same meal with a cereal that would tend to make for not too *great an* excess of starch but more of the *gluten* with same; as the uncut or unpolished rice, or the cracked wheat or rolled whole wheat, or the rye or the oat. Any or all of these *combined* would be added at the same meal with the vegetable juices, you see.

Evenings—a well balance between the green raw vegetables and more of the body-building foods; such as lamb, liver, tripe, or the like, that make for the body-building forces.

276–8

Hence we would have the stimulating foods; such as:

Mornings—Whole wheat, Maltex and such cereals.

Noons—we would have the Jerusalem artichoke at least three times a week; then salsify soups or parsnips, lentils and the green beans of leafy vegetables—these all in their combinations.

Evenings—preferably broths that are a combination of vegetables and meats.

Never any fried foods. Never any of those foods that carry too much starches. And all the bread should be either black bread or whole wheat bread.

Do these CONSISTENTLY, and we will find we may bring the better conditions for this body.

1454–1

And then, to show the variety of approaches—and yet how consistent the Cayce material is on many items of the diet—the next six extracts of the readings offer six different menus:

As to the matter of diet, we would keep rather those foods that are of an alkaline nature for the body (for it is necessary for the diet to be considered with this body). This may be used as an outline, though not these foods alone—see?

Mornings—citrus fruit juices or stewed fruits, or the glutens of the whole wheat or cooked cereal; but do not use citrus fruits *and* cereal at the same meal. It would be preferable that these be given in small quantities at the time but given the more often.

Noons—preferably a liquid or semi-liquid diet, such as would be found in beef juices or broths or vegetable juices. Only take the beef juices in the middle of the day, not at other meals; not the broth of the beef, but the beef *juices*.

Evenings—first we would have rather the stimulations from light wine, or that which will form from the vine—or of the grape; a form of the necessary quantity of alcohol that will make for an activity with the gastric juices of the stomach *as* these are being taken, see? A well-balanced vegetable and meat diet in the evening; but do not include beef or pork meat of *any* nature. Lamb or lamb stew, with the vegetables that will easily assimilate, will be well; or fish or fowl.

728–1

And we would change the diet as into *this* way and manner; of course, this being merely an outline that may be altered to suit the tastes of the body:

Mornings—citrus fruit or, the more often, stewed fruits—which should include, at least three or four times each week, that of rhubarb.

We would also take at the morning meals, after the citrus fruit or with the stewed fruit, psyllium seed. Two teaspoonfuls in four tablespoonfuls of boiling water. Allow to jell before it is eaten.

Occasionally it would be found well, too, that the yolk of egg be added; not too hard cooked, or cooked *hard* and then mashed or mixed with any ingredient that makes it more palatable for the body. But do not include the white of egg in the diet, just take the yolk.

However, to be sure, there may be

many periods when the white and the yolk may be taken; *especially* will this be found helpful if it is taken in the middle of the morning with dried milk or such properties that make for an egg and milk drink, see? As malted milk, dried milk, or the like. To this there should be added, also, some stimuli—either wine or spirits frumenti, or beer, or malt, that will aid in the *digestion* through the system.

Noons—any of the vegetable juices or soups, or the juices of *meats* that may be prepared; but do not *mix* or have large quantities of meats or *greases* in preparing the noon-day meal, see? At this meal there should be a good deal of butter, a good deal of brown bread, or the like, taken.

Evenings—the whole vegetable diet, well-balanced; and at least three or four times each week the calf's liver, tripe, or the like, should be taken. Pig knuckles, also, are well; *preferably* these should be fresh rather than the pickled variety, for little or none of those that are of the acidic acid base should be taken for the body, save when *some* vegetables are taken that may be prepared with very small quantities of same.

313–5

In the diets we would follow rather the alkaline-reacting foods; or this would be as an outline—though this does not mean that no other foods are to be taken:

Mornings—preferably citrus fruit juices, or fruits, or cereals that are not too much of the roughage (as the crushed whole wheat). But do not take cereals *and* citrus fruit juices at the same meal:

Let one meal each day be preferably only of raw vegetables. These may be taken in the manners that are the more palatable to the taste, for better assimilation.

Beware of too much starches; as potatoes or white breads. Not too great a quantity of sweets, but these may be taken in moderation—the *natural* sweets are preferable (such as honey, and the sweets that are contained in fruits and vegetables).

1088–1

In the diets—these, as indicated, are the more important; and these would be rather strict for the first two or three months anyway. And then gradually may the change be made to a nominal diet. These would be as an outline, and rather stick to these.

Mornings—dry cereals about three times a week; cooked cereals once or twice a week. This should be *whole wheat,* and with milk—or milk and cream preferably on all of these. Dry cereals take fruit on same; these may be orange, bananas or strawberries or peaches or any of the fruits or the berries.

Noons—nothing save raw vegetables.

About three to four o'clock in the afternoon drink an ounce of red wine with black bread.

Evenings—well-cooked vegetables of the leafy variety. Not a great amount of meats. Never any fried foods of *any* kind. Boiled onions should be in almost every evening meal. The meats would be fowl, fish, or lamb.

Do these and we will find conditions will be near to normal.

1164–1

Mornings—either fresh fruits or melon or dry cereal, or the citrus fruit juices, but do not mix *any* of these together. With the fruit may be taken a little crisp bacon and a coddled or poached egg, but no fried eggs.

Noons—rather the green, fresh, raw vegetables, even when there are the activities in school let the lunch be rather of the lettuce and tomato sandwich, but as much of the green, fresh, raw vegetables as may be eaten. Such as lettuce, celery, carrots, tomatoes, peppers, beans, radishes, radish tops, turnips, turnip tops, and *especially* onions—preferably, though, the onions would be eaten before retiring at night. This, as we find, will overcome those tendencies for the activities of the kidneys, and adjust same better.

Evenings—either liver (as meats), fish, tripe, pigs' feet and ears, souse or the like, and green vegetables that are well cooked. And each evening let a portion of the meal be of *boiled* onions, that are boiled in their *own* juices; *not* in water. Those eaten before retiring preferably should be raw; not large quantities, but small quantities, for these carry a vitamin and the elements necessary for the dilation of not only the pulmonary activity but for the juices—gastric juices of the stomach and assimilating forces of the body.

308-2

Q-8: Please give the diet I should follow.
A-8: Keep the diet rather alkaline. That means not too much meat or too much starch, or too much of *any* of those things that *produce* acidity. But don't make self as subject to a diet. Rather subject the diet to self, by self's activity; that is, keep a normal well-balanced diet, but no hog meats ever—unless a little crisp breakfast bacon at times. Preferably, when meats are taken, fish, fowl, lamb, or mutton.

574-1

You can begin to see that diets are tremendously unique and individually formulated. So make a creative start on the attempt and see what happens with your body, as you begin the process of balancing those life support systems better than they have ever been coordinated before. It can be done.

The following lists will help you in becoming acquainted with the commonsense rules of eating that emerge from our own experience and the body of the Edgar Cayce readings on diet and health.

1. Alkaline-forming Foods

Choose 80 percent (four out of five servings) daily from these foods:

Vegetables (cooked or raw—includes soups)

Artichokes, green and Jerusalem
Asparagus (near neutral)
Beans, fresh or dried (green, lima,
    wax, soy, etc.)
Beets and beet tops
Cabbage, red and white
Carob
Carrots
Cauliflower
Celery
Eggplant
Endive
Green peas
Kale
Lettuce, leafy best
Mushrooms
Mustard greens
Okra
Olives
Onions, white
Oyster plant
Parsley
Parsnips
Peppers, green
Poke greens
Potatoes, sweet
Potatoes, white (skin and cooking
    water best)
Radishes

Rutabaga
Salsify (oyster plant)
Spinach
Sprouts
String beans
Tomatoes (vine ripe)
Turnips and greens
Watercress

Fruits (fresh, dried, cooked, or juiced)

Apples (eat alone)
Apricots
Avocados
Bananas (tree ripe)
Berries (except cranberry)
Cherries
Dates
Figs
Grapes
Grapefruit
Guava
Limes
Melons
Oranges
Papaya
Peaches
Pears
Pineapple
Pomegranate
Prunes
Quince
Raisins
Most other fruits

Milk and Milk Products

Buttermilk
Cream
Milk (whole, skim, raw, evaporated, etc.)
Yogurt

Miscellaneous Alkaline

Desserts, such as ice cream, Jell-O
Lentils (near neutral)
Oils, olive and peanut (near neutral) most
    recommended
Pumpernickel
Sweeteners, honey best (slightly acid in comb)
Water

2. Acid-forming Foods

Choose 20 percent daily from these foods:

Fish (baked, boiled, broiled, etc.—never fried)
Seafood of all kinds highly stressed, including
    shellfish (clams, oysters, lobster)

Grains and Their Products

Bread (corn, sourdough, rye, whole wheat—
    toasted best)
Cereals, especially cooked (steel-cut oats, cracked
    wheat, wheat and barley, corn, rice, wheat
    germ)
Crackers (whole wheat, rye)
Pancakes (whole wheat, buckwheat, corn rice)
Rice (brown)

Meats (baked boiled, broiled, etc.—never fried)

Beef, lean (well done)—beef juice
    best part (see BEEF JUICE recipe
    on page 226)
Lamb
Poultry—chicken, turkey, etc.
Wild game

Miscellaneous Acid

Beef juice (near neutral)
Butter (near natural)
Cake, cookies, pastry
Cheese, cheddar and cottage
Corn, sweet
Cranberries
Eggs (yolk preferred)
Margarine
Nuts (almonds and filberts
    preferred—near neutral—
    peanuts, English walnuts, Brazil
    nuts)

3. Beverages Recommended

Milk and milk drinks
Cereal drinks (Postum)
Ovaltine
Cocoa (not preferred)
Eggnog (yolk only, add a little
    apple brandy if desired)
Malted milk
Teas, herbal (various—usually
    medicinal)

Vegetable juices, raw and cooked
  (spinach, beet, carrot, onion,
  sauerkraut, tomato)
Water (six to eight glasses daily,
  best pure or boiled)
Warm milk and honey—nightcap

4. Choose These Foods in Moderation

Coffee, black (sometimes avoid)
Desserts, using only honey to
  sweeten
Apples, baked
Custard
Fruit, all kinds
Gelatin desserts
Ice Cream
Junket
Honey—comb often stressed
Salt (iodized, kelp, sea or
  vegetable) and other seasonings
Tea, no milk or cream (sometimes
  avoid)

5. Avoid These Foods
  as Much as Possible

Animal fats
Apples, raw
Bananas (for arthritis and related
  conditions)
Beer
Candy
Cane sugar (brown and beet
  sugars are a little better)

Carbonated beverages
Condiments
Fried foods
Hard liquor
Pastry (pie, etc.)
Pork (except crisp bacon
   occasionally)
Raw or rare meats
Strawberries (for arthritis and
   related conditions)
White flour and its products

6. Stress These Combinations

Mummy Food: Figs, dates, and cornmeal, as a
   cleanser and "spiritual food" (see MUMMY FOOD
   recipe on page 245).
Gelatin with raw vegetables (aids assimilation of
   their nutrients)
Orange, grapefruit, or pineapple with lemon or
   lime juice (more balanced)
Red wine with dark bread (occasionally in
   afternoon as a blood and bodybuilder)

7. Avoid These Combinations (too acid forming
   or very difficult to digest)

Citrus and cereal or other starches
Citrus and milk (and probably all milk products)
Coffee or tea with milk or cream
Fruits and vegetables at the same meal
Meat or cheese with starch
Oysters and alcohol
Raw apples and other foods
Starch combinations

Sweets (sugar) and starch
Vegetables cooked with meat or meat fats
Yams or potatoes with meats or fats

8. Typical Sample Menus

BREAKFAST: Alternate these options: (1) citrus fruit; (2) cooked (or dry) cereal, served with a little honey, milk, or cream, fresh or cooked fruit (not citrus) if desired; (3) eggs with whole wheat toast, a little crisp bacon if desired; (4) pancakes, whole grain, served with butter and a little honey. Cereal beverage preferred.

LUNCH: Raw vegetable salad with dressing (no vinegar) or mayonnaise. Serve with soup and whole grain bread or crackers if desired. Fruit salads may be alternated. Beverage of choice.

DINNER: Cooked vegetables (three grown above ground to one below ground) served with fish, poultry, or lamb as desired. Beverage of choice.

BETWEEN MEALS: Egg nog, fruit and fruit juices, nuts, vegetables juices.

9. Special Fruit Diets

The next three diets have been suggested in the Cayce readings to bring about specific changes in the body. Sometimes we may feel upset and in need of balancing, or perhaps we may want to drop a few pounds or cleanse our bodies. On occasion we may be under a great deal of stress and cleansing or balancing becomes a necessity. These diets have been helpful in such circumstances.

BANANAS AND BUTTERMILK: A two- to three-day balancing diet. Eat only bananas and buttermilk.

APPLE DIET: A three-day cleansing diet. Eat only apples (type with bumps on bottom, delicious for example)—as many as desired. On evening of third day, follow with 1 tablespoon to ½ cup olive oil. Drink plenty of water, a little coffee, or a cereal drink (no milk or cream) if desired.

GRAPE DIET: A three- to four-day diet. Eat only large amounts of grapes, preferable Concord.

10. Food Preparation Suggestions

Choose when available: Fresh, locally grown foods, vine- or tree-ripened foods.

Cook vegetables in plain water or Patapar paper; season just before serving.

Cook vegetables separately, then combine.

Use a pressure cooker to preserve vitamins.

Try to use glass and enamel utensils. Avoid aluminum.

11. About Jerusalem Artichokes

Jerusalem artichokes are tuberous vegetables low in starch, recommended generally and specifically in the readings as a source of insulin (although they contain inulin, not insulin). For most individuals, an egg-sized artichoke eaten once weekly is sufficient. In cases of illness such as diabetes, consult the readings for directions. Eat raw or cook in Patapar paper.

12. For More Information see Chapter 7: Commonsense Odds and Ends and References for Further Reading.

SELF-EVALUATION QUIZ

HOW DO YOU SCORE?

WHEN YOU ARE SHOPPING	YES	NO
1. Do you avoid buying refined foods such as white flour or sugar?	_____	_____
2. Are you aware that locally grown foods are better for you, especially grown in your own backyard?	_____	_____
3. Do you avoid buying canned or bottled foods whenever possible?	_____	_____
4. Are you in the habit of checking labels for preservatives and other chemicals in the food you buy?	_____	_____
5. Do you choose natural foods in preference to processed foods?	_____	_____
6. Do you have a good variety of foods in your diet, trying new vegetables, fruits, and recipes?	_____	_____
7. Do you use fresh vegetables often?	_____	_____

WHEN YOU ARE COOKING	YES	NO
1. Do you serve your fruits and vegetables nearest their natural state of preserve nutrients (i.e., cooking as little as possible)? Do you avoid soaking them?	_____	_____
2. Do you avoid cooking in aluminum utensils?	_____	_____
3. Do you steam your vegetables rather than boiling them?	_____	_____
4. Do you wash your fresh foods before eating?	_____	_____
5. Do you avoid FRYING foods?	_____	_____

WHEN YOU ARE EATING	YES	NO
1. Do you chew your food well before swallowing?	_____	_____
2. Do you avoid getting up once you have sat down to eat and do you take your time to enjoy your meals?	_____	_____
3. When you are angry or upset do you put off eating until you calm down?	_____	_____

	YES	NO

4. Are you aware that vitamins and minerals from foods are more easily assimilated and therefore better for you than those from manufactured sources? _____ _____

5. Are you aware that some foods (although they may be good for you separately) should not be combined at the same meal? _____ _____
   For example:
   a. Citrus and whole grain products.
   b. Starches and sweets (such as pies).
   c. Coffee or tea with cream or milk.

SCORE YOURSELF

1. If you marked yes seventeen times, you're just about perfect!

2. If yes was marked thirteen to sixteen times, you're doing great and need little improvement.

3. If your score is yes seven to twelve times, you need to work on your shopping, your cooking, and your eating.

4. If you score yes only one to six times, your life-style as far as food is concerned needs a lot of readjustment. Keep on reading!

ADDITIONAL CAYCE READINGS ABOUT DIET

It is always helpful to go to some of the original Cayce material so that you can understand better how he approached the preparation and selection of foods to be used by the human body. The following selections will give you additional help and perhaps some fresh ideas that will be useful to you.

Q-3: Please suggest things to be stressed and things to be avoided in the diet.
A-3: AVOID too much combinations of starches. Do not take a combination of potatoes, meat, white bread, macaroni, or cheese at the same meal; no two of these at any one meal, though they each may be taken separately at other times, or as a lunch or a part of a meal. Avoid raw meats, or rare meats—that are not well cooked. Not too much EVER of any hog meat. Have plenty of vegetables, and especially one meal each day should include some raw or uncooked vegetables. But here, too, combinations must be kept in line. Do not take onions and radishes at the same meal with celery and lettuce, though either of these may be taken at different times, see?

2732–1

Q-3: Specify diet.
A-3: Keep the alkaline reaction. That the best: Beware of condiments and of those conditions that overtax the system in *any* direction, especially of those that create an *acid* condition in the system, for better blood builds in an *alkaline* reaction.

337–11

Q-6: What diet should I follow?
A-6: The diet has been outlined. In the milks, use the malted or dry milks rather than those in which there is so much of the fat or animal fat. For the body has in its meditation, in its activities, made for changes in the vibratory forces of the body itself. And animal fats then become a hardship upon the general system.

But keep for a normal balance of the alkaline reaction. Not that no meats should ever be taken; for fowl, fish, mutton, or lamb are well. But other types are not so well. Wild game in its regular season is well. Keep a well-balanced vegetable diet, making for the correct balance; that is, not that it becomes rote, but watch self. If too great a combination of such as peas, lentils, beans, carrots, becomes a hardship or produces—as from the natural coloring, the natural manner in which these are prepared—irritation through the creating of an effluvium in the bloodstream, it is not that the food *value* itself is wrong; possibly it's the preparation! These should be noted and watched by the body. For all of these especially as indicated are well for the body, though they do make disturbances in their preparation. There is a vast difference in the effect they create upon the body itself when prepared differently! For carrots, both raw and cooked, are helpful—and helpful elements of a special nature that are especially good for the body. But there should be almost as many eaten raw as there are cooked! And when cooked, *not* with a lot of others, but in their *own* juices! For these are the better.

1000–12

Q-6: Is my system in an alkaline or acid condition, and what foods will provide proper balance?

A-6: There have been the tendencies toward an acidity, and especially from those conditions that have been described in times before as to the leakages in the intestinal tract, in the thinned walls, and those tendencies for the circulation to carry this in an improper way and manner for the eliminations; producing the rash and those conditions—which tendency has existed for some time. [Psoriasis tendency?] Hence there is the *natural* tendency for the body to react to acids. While in the present we have this tendency, as we find, there is a much better balance than has been indicated here before. And there should be, as we have maintained for this body and for others, a tendency toward more of the alkaline-reacting foods; for when there is the tendency toward an alkaline system there is less effect of cold and congestion. Adhere to the alkaline-reacting diets, meal, or one period each day, or at least two or three days apart, have these wholly raw. Have less of the sweets, or not too great a quantity. Naturally, there should be sweets that tend to make for the proper distribution of sugar for the system, for sugars—to be sure—supply not only heat but also the proper balance for proper fermentation, as do starches; but if these arise more from fruits and vegetables rather than the addition of cane sugar into the body, it will be much the better, for then less acidity arises from same. To be sure, there should be sufficient of starch and of the alkaline reactions to produce proper fermentation, or the proper character of the alcohol that is so necessary in preserving the calorie content, in a manner; though the calories may be made too high, but the activity of the necessary vital forces that act with the hemoglobin and in the urea of the blood itself. Hence an alkaline diet, as has been indicated—or as may be indicated from charts of same, would be the correct way and manner. Do not have overeating at any time. Keep a well balance. And, as some have very much commented on or maintained, if meats are to be taken in any quantity don't eat a lot of starch with same; if there's to be a lot of sweets taken, don't eat a lot of starch or proteins either with it; but keep them well balanced. See?

270–33

Q-3: What foods should I avoid?
A-3: Rather is it the combination of foods that makes for disturbance with most physical bodies, as it would with this.

In the activities of the body in its present surroundings, those tending toward the greater alkaline reaction are preferable. Hence avoid combinations where corn, potatoes, rice, spaghetti, or the like are taken all at the same meal. Some combinations of these at the meal are very good, but all of these tend to make for too great a quantity of starch—especially if any meat is taken at such a meal. If no meat is taken, these make quite a difference. For the activities of the gastric flow of the digestive system are the requirements of one reaction in the gastric flow for starch and another for proteins, or for the activities of the carbohydrates as combined with starches of this nature—

especially in the manner in which they are prepared. Then, in the combinations, do not eat great
quantities of starch with the proteins or meats. If
sweets and meats are taken at the same meal,
these are preferable to starches. Of course, small
quantities of breads with sweets are alright, but
do not have large quantities of same. These are
merely warnings.

Then, do not combine also the reacting acid
fruits with starches, other than *whole wheat
bread!* that is, citrus fruits, oranges, apples,
grapefruit, limes, or lemons or even tomato juices.
And do not have cereals (which contain the greater
quantity of starch than most) at the same meal
with the citrus fruits. These we will find will make
for quite a variation in the *feelings* and in the
activity of the body, if these suggestions are ad-
hered to.

416–9

Keep the eliminations near normal, with
the diets toward a tendency of the alkaline-reacting rather than large quantities
of meats or sweets—but these taken in
their proper proportions. Eat the sweets
rather with meats than with breads. Vegetables are the preferable for the body.

533–11

*Q-2: What can I do to avoid losing so much
weight? Outline the proper diet.*
A-2: Those foods, now, that are the body-building;
as starches and proteins, if these are taken without other food values that make for the combina-

99

tions that produce distress or disorder; that is, not quantities of starches and proteins combined, you see, but these taken one at one meal and one at another will be most helpful. As potatoes, whether white or the yam activity with butter, should not be taken with fats or meats; but using these as a portion of one meal with *fruits* or vegetables is well. When meats are taken, use mutton, fowl, or the like, and do not have heavy starches with same—but preferably fruits or vegetables. These will be found to be much more preferable. Fresh fruits, nuts, and the like, taken as a part of a meal at different periods, as the body finds that the system is able to handle same, are much preferable to combining so many in one period.

805-2

Then, we would outline this as a diet; in the present:

Mornings—citrus fruits or cereals, but not both at the same meal. Fresh fruits or stewed fruits, any of these may be taken—but not both at once, see?

A little very crisp bacon—not burned, but crisp—may be taken occasionally.

Coddled eggs, or prepared in any manner just so they are not fried in grease. Scrambled in butter would be very well, but the more often it would be better for them to be taken without the white; that is, only using the yolk.

Whole wheat toast. Not too great an amount of butter, but a small amount now may be taken.

Ovaltine or any cereal drink; a little

coffee occasionally, but use brown sugar or honey for the sweetening—and do not sweeten too much.

Noons—as near as possible, keep to brown whole wheat bread, or Graham bread, or toasted rye bread, with whole green vegetables; or vegetable and egg sandwiches may be taken, see? These would consist of such as lettuce, celery, tomatoes (with mayonnaise), tomato juice, or the like.

Do not combine tomato juice with any citrus fruit juices, for they work toward a combination of proteins and elements that work against one another.

Evenings—whole vegetables, well cooked with little meats; occasionally fowl, lamb and fish may be taken—and may be found to work well, if not too much of these is taken.

Just eat sufficient to supply the appetite, but don't overload the stomach.

306—3

In the matter of the diet, keep same well balanced as to an alkaline and an acid reaction. Do not combine at the same meals potatoes, white bread, spaghetti, or macaroni. Do not combine any two of these in the same meal. Eat rather potatoes in the jacket and the peel rather than the pulp; the salts of these are most beneficial to the very activities of the body. Do not take cereals and citrus fruit juices on the same day. Keep a balance well with the sweets or carbohydrates and meats. These combined together for the body are the better, as with fish or fowl or lamb—that is preferable to roast or other types of meat; though, to be sure, breakfast bacon may be taken if it is prepared very crisp without much of the fat or grease in same.

23–3

Mornings—either the citrus fruit juices OR cooked or dry cereal, but DO NOT take the citrus fruit juices AND the cereal—either dry OR cooked—at the same meal! With either there may be taken whole wheat toast, buttered, with either a cereal drink or with coffee—provided the coffee is used without milk or cream, though sugar may be used in same if so desired. Occasionally change to honey and waffles or buckwheat or corn cakes, with a little butter if so desired. No other sweets in the morning meal.

Noons—either the raw vegetable combinations with a salad dressing, or vegetable juices that may be either chilled or hot—as desired. In this meal there may be taken gelatin or Jell-O, or the like, as a dessert.

Evenings—fish, fowl, or lamb, with vegetables that are preferably cooked in their OWN juices, or in Patapar Paper, AND their JUICES taken as a part of the diet with the vegetables, see?

Do not fry foods; these may be broiled or roasted or boiled, see?

1623–2

6

--- ✳ ---

Food as Medicine

GENERAL FACTORS

When I started the practice of medicine in 1948, I felt triumphant when one of my patients would recover after an inflamed appendix was removed—or when I gave some sulfa tablets to a young lad suffering with tonsillitis, and he also got well. I thought it made me the "healer," and obviously that was highly self-satisfying.

What I didn't understand at that time was that the surgeon's knife only removed the offending organ; the body's immune system and its co-operating other organs and systems really did the healing. The appendectomy was simply the *incentive* that stimulated the healing of the body, and the removal of the toxins allowed the body to recover. The case of the tonsillitis was basically the same.

In my work with the Cayce material over the past three decades, I've become aware that none of us really does the healing—it is that wonderful ability within the body, the Life Force, that brings it about. And we can stop the healing by putting up the barriers of resistance, rebellion, rejection, or defiance if we wish. It is a rather remarkable insight, for it forced me to reevaluate my stance with my patients.

Gladys and I began to look at the healing of the human body as a multilevel, physiological event that involved the body, certainly; the mind, for the will and choice had to be there; and the spirit, for without that there is no life.

The first step, logically, in helping the body to recover from an illness is to give the individual the kind of a diet that will start reversing the destruction that has been going on and begin the rebuilding needed for health to come about again.

From the food, the intestinal system and the digestive organs need to create building blocks that can then be taken to the various parts of the body where dying cells can be replaced in the process that Cayce looked at as "coagulation."

In addition to the process of rebuilding, it is necessary to stimulate back into action processes within the body that have lost their normal abilities. These processes are physiological activities and coordinations between organs and systems that have been put into disarray through stress or by the disobedience of physical laws of the human body. These abnormalities were basic in causing illness in the very beginning, so it is only reasonable that they need to be put back onto the straight and narrow once again.

Exercise, for instance, will increase the oxygen intake in the lungs and circulation and generally alkalinize the system through the adrenal activity that has been called into action. The adrenal also has the ability to burn up toxins and in that way create a healthier condition within the body. Another instance of physiological change is found when a diet of fresh vegetables and vegetable juice is followed for several days. The effect is to alkalinize the entire body, to an extent. It increases the immune activity and protects against infections. It would be hard to catch a cold while on such a diet.

Sometimes medicines are given to help this out. Cayce talked about this in a number of his readings, for he felt that the nearer we can come to treating the body naturally, the better off we will be. This reading deals with that concept:

> . . . In those activities that have been given [such as the diet and correction of eliminations], we find we are adding elements that are as incentives for the *system* to create that within the body itself. While oft we find in the administration of medicinal properties, whether they be of the mineral or vegetable forces, if those things administered are habit-forming, or if they are those things that tend to take the place *of* the activities of organs in the system, they eventually prove to be detrimental. For the body builds with that which is supplied it *through* the assimilating system.
>
> 1014–2

The food, then, might be considered a medicine, if we can look at medicine as being that which helps normalize the body. And, as Cayce pointed out so often, the better method of restoring the body back to normal is that which nature supplies.

Foods can often bring about better eliminations—a process that is essential to health and that can cause difficulty with the assimilations of the body if not functioning properly. Much good can come from a simple alkaline-reacting diet at times:

> If we will use the diets that are alkaline-creating in the system, we find we will make for the proper eliminations—especially if there will be the greater activity of the body; and we will overcome the tendency for nervousness, for the accumulations in the lymph circulation to make for blemishes or red spots or blackheads, and the tendencies for the inability of the body to concentrate. For with a torpid liver, with the acidity in the system, all of these make for pressures upon the nervous energies of the body.
>
> 361–5

And Cayce also pointed out that it is not just the digestive tract that gets involved in the natural way of healing, but:

> Those things that will work then with the digestive forces, those that work with the nerve energies, those that make for keeping a balance in these physical ways, as we find would be the more preferable

and helpful to the body—with the precautions mentally and physically in its exercise.

694–3

Remember, the body rebuilds and replenishes itself continually. What portion would be the more active in its changes than those that *are* channels for those very changes—the *digestive* forces of the body; the lungs, the liver, the heart, the digestive system, the pancreas, the spleen? All of these change the more often, so that when it is ordinarily termed that the body has changed each atom in seven years, these organs have changed almost *seven times* during those seven years!

796–2

NERVE AND BODY-BUILDING DIETS

Many factors—family arguments, financial worries, job pressures, too many fast foods—contribute to the breakdown of the nervous system, the organs, and the body itself. The rebuilding process needs to be addressed at some point during our lives and we make stabs at it every now and then. We may change jobs or we may find peace within the home or we may take steps toward improving our diet. It is well to know what can be done in the way of dietary changes that might be most helpful. This is especially true in regard to the nervous system, the tensions, the lack of restful sleeping:

The diets should be those that are easily assimilated, and that are nerve building; that is, a great deal of green vegetables—or at least one meal each day should be of green vegetables, though mayonnaise or oil dressings may be used with same.

629-1

Q-4: *What is a nerve building diet?*
A-4: Those of the celery, radish, those of the green vegetables, in tomatoes. Those of the active forces in these are the nerve building, with those of the *juices*—but not the flesh—of animal [beef juice].

255-3

Cayce gave a reading for a woman who had digestive problems. He saw the walls of the duodenum thickened, gravel in the gallbladder, the inability of the liver to function properly or to coordinate with the kidneys, and "poisons" being brought into the bloodstream from both the liver and the kidneys. Apparently, the liver and kidneys were not able to eliminate the metabolites which they were duty-bound to remove from the system, and this in turn had caused this woman's problem. We had this to say about her diet:

In the diet, let the foods taken be rather bodybuilding. This would be as an outline:
Mornings—cereals or citrus fruits, but do not take these at the same meal. At least two or three times each week we

would have the whole wheat cereal, not too thoroughly cooked but cooked sufficient that the vitamins are preserved in same. It may be taken with a little milk, but not too much sugar.

In the middle of the morning we would take beef juices; not beef, but the *juice*—that may be prepared every three or four days. The quantity would be about a tablespoonful, but taken in very small quantities; that is, little sips at a time—a tablespoonful each day should give strength and vitality to the body.

Noons—rather the juices of vegetables that are cooked in their *own* juices, or in Patapar paper. These may be combined with a little of the vegetables; or we may alter these to the use of raw green vegetables combined as a salad, including such as cabbage, lettuce, celery, tomatoes, carrots, spinach, peppers, radish, mustard. Any or all of these; not too great a quantity but sufficient to satisfy the appetites.

In the middle of the afternoon we would have rather the dry milk, or buttermilk or the like; not in large quantities.

Evenings—well-cooked vegetables themselves. Very little meat should be taken; only fowl, lamb, or the like.

855–1

To another woman who was just twenty-one years old, he suggested that she take a breakfast similar to that listed in the reading just given and

a lunch composed of raw green vegetables or vegetable juices or a combination of both. Then he had
this to say about her evening meal:

> Evenings—rather vegetables that carry a
> well-balance in iron, silicon, and espe-
> cially of the natures that make for body-
> building, or the Vitamin D; as we find in
> vegetables of the nature that are cooked
> in their *own* broth or their own activity,
> so that the vitamins are maintained in
> same. Fish, fowl, lamb, pig knuckle, or
> the like are *well*, for the bodybuilding, at
> the various periods. Not too much of
> sweets at *any* time. These, if taken,
> should be rather with those of the nature
> that makes for bodybuilding, rather than
> those that act upon the pancreas action
> in the system.
>
> 275–42

A breast-feeding mother sought Cayce's advice
on her diet—what would be best for the infant?

Q-7: Any advice as to diet of the mother?
A-7: Keep a diet well-balanced or well-rounded in
iron, nitrogen, and the necessary bone structural
forces in the activities that arise from such diets.
Milk, a good vegetable diet; not acid forming foods,
not too heavy of meats—but a well-rounded, well-
balanced diet.

928–1

DIET TO PREVENT A COLD

When you are exposed to a cold, a normal, alkaline-reacting diet should be kept at all times. You should eat a lot of fresh fruits, though citrus fruits should not be combined with cereals at the same meal. This combination creates a digestive disturbance and the body does not benefit from the food. Raw green vegetables should be part of the diet, and you should go easy on meats. Your normal diet, proven over a period of time, is probably the best course to take. Cayce suggested for one person:

> . . . Keep the diet tending more toward the alkaline-reacting foods and we will find that through the coming season there will be little or no cold, and that the throat, the nasal passages, and the general system will keep in a much better *responsive* way and manner.

> 584—5

Q-2: What should be done to build resistance against colds?
A-2: Keep the body more alkaline. This may be done by taking food values that are more alkaline in their reaction, and occasionally—say once a week (but do not take it every day)—take a small quantity of plain baking soda; using Glyco-Thymoline as a mouthwash, and occasionally swallow a few drops, for it's an intestinal antiseptic—and there is none better for keeping the eliminations throughout the body, tending toward alkalinity in the alimentary canal—where most disorders arise.

413—4

THIRTEEN DIETARY SUGGESTIONS
FOR SPECIAL AILMENTS

It should be repeated that nutritional measures alone do not really bring healing to the body—and it was the wholeness of healing that Cayce tried to instill in each of those who came to him for readings. It *always* involved the whole being—the mind, with its power to choose; the body, where the difficulties lay and where changes needed to come about; and the spirit, which brings life to the body.

However, if you are interested in making a significant change, if you will work with your physical body through exercises and those things that may be necessary for rebuilding, then the diet you choose can be very specific in helping you regain health.

For instance, exercise must be taken within the limits the body dictates when a person has arthritis. Peanut oil massages of affected joints, series of castor oil packs applied to the abdomen, and improvement of attitudes and emotional patterns are all needed to see real betterment in the joint structure. But the alkaline-reacting diet is a basic and perhaps most important item to bring healing to the whole body when a person has arthritis.

Since Cayce's death, many efforts have been made to provide some practical help for those who have been interested in his material, especially where diets can be helpful. Much information regarding foods and their benefits, special diets for different conditions, and ways to approach healing an illness of the body can be found by reading those works in the *Bibliography* section at the back of this book.

The following thirteen dietary suggestions were chosen from workups I have done in the past, from information in the *Physician's Reference Notebook* (1983), and from my understanding of the Cayce readings themselves.

You'll find several themes being repeated throughout the recommendations. Maintaining an alkaline diet seems to be a matter of course. Also a matter of course is avoiding those combinations of foods that cause difficulty in the upper intestinal tract—meat and starch, for instance, which call for opposing responses in the stomach and duodenum.

These things make for certain patterns of constructive eating that can become habitual with most of us, and thus *prevent* a problem from arising—which, in turn, can prolong our lives. Then we have to remember that we are here for a purpose, after all—and what is it? Let's recall to our minds often the advice Edgar Cayce gave to one such seeker:

> For, all healing comes from the one source. And whether there is the application of foods, exercise, medicine, or even the knife—it is to bring the consciousness of the forces within the body that aid in reproducing themselves—the awareness of creative or God forces.

> 2696-1

113

1. Acne

1. Take a yeast cake or a packet of dry yeast and blend into eight ounces of tomato or V-8 Juice. (You may use other juices if you wish.) A dash of lime juice and Worcestershire sauce adds a little tang in the V-8 mix. Take once a day for ten days. Then stop for a week and repeat.
2. Obtain some Coca-Cola syrup from a soda fountain. Take one teaspoonful in a glass of *plain* water once or twice a day.
3. No chocolate, sugars, ice cream, pastries, pie, or candy.
4. No carbonated drinks, including diet drinks. No beer or ale.
5. No pork or ham. *Crisp* bacon allowed, however.
6. Limit starches to *one* source per meal: bread, rice, potato, spaghetti, or corn, for instance. No white bread should be eaten.
7. No fried foods. This includes corn chips and potato chips.
8. Vegetables are good for you. Have plenty of salads, vegetable soup, and cooked vegetables. Salad dressing is all right.
9. Fruits are fine in season except raw apples, strawberries, and bananas.
10. In the meats, especially recommended are lamb, fish, and fowl. *Lean* beef is all right.
11. Milk (skim), eggs, and cheese are allowed.

2. Arthritis

Nearly all cases of arthritis fall into one of two general classifications, which are relatively easily differentiated, although poorly understood.

Atrophic—more commonly called rheumatoid—arthritis has also been given the names proliferative arthritis or arthritis deformans. This disease is characterized by inflammatory changes in the synovial membranes of the joints and in the structures around the joints, and by atrophy and loss of calcium in the bones. In the early stages there is a migratory swelling and stiffness of the joints, with a rather typical fusiform swelling of the finger joints. Later on there is deformity with ankylosis (or freezing of the joints) and frequently an ulnar deviation of the fingers as a sign of this disease. Nodules under the skin are frequent in these patients, and usually the disease is found beginning in young people, more commonly the female than the male. Present are anemia, chronic emaciation, loss of calcium in the bone structures, and the patient is rather severely and chronically ill.

Hypertrophic arthritis gives an entirely different picture. This has been called more commonly osteoarthritis and is known as degenerative or senescent arthritis. In this disease process there is generally no inflammation and no spreading or migratory type of joint involvement. Rather than a loss of calcium, there is a calcium buildup. An example of this is the so-called "Heberden's nodes"—a swelling and buildup of calcium about the base of the terminal phalanges of both hands. In osteoarthritis, there are calcific spurs and there is deformity of the joints, but never ankylosis and rarely, if ever, the ulnar deviation of the fingers such as is found in atrophic arthritis. (There are other types of arthritis not quite so common. The arthritis associated with rheumatic fever and those found with various inflammatory diseases constitute the majority of this group. Gout might be listed in a separate classification.)

Avoid: Hog meat, fats, fried foods, white potatoes, carbonated drinks, coffee, tea, other stimulants, salt, bananas, starchy foods such as macaroni and cheese, sweets, pastries, pies, cakes, commercialized ice creams, candies, and cabbage (which is high in calcium).

Fruits: Stewed fruits, prunes, raisins, berries, gooseberries; citrus, when taken alone, is a good eliminant; also cooked apples, pears, plums, and figs.

Vegetables: Those that make vegetable salts, which combine a well-balanced amount of vegetables—turnips, eggplant, leaf lettuce, celery, carrots (eat daily, often with gelatin), watercress, beets, onions, radishes, mustard greens, beet tops, and yellow yams (no white potatoes). Leafy vegetables are better than bulbous because they help eliminations.

Grains: Whole grains, corn bread, brown bread (no white bread).

116

Meat: Mostly fish and seafoods (oysters, shellfish); some fowl, wild game; some liver (not fried); lamb; and beef juice (see the BEEF JUICE recipe in Chapter 9). No beef or other red meats or hog meats.

Drink: Slippery elm bark is good in water because it cleanses. American saffron tea is also good—a pinch in a cup of boiling water. No carbonated drinks; avoid stimulants such as coffee or tea; and take a glass of milk occasionally in the evening with half a teaspoon of honey.

Precautions: Don't eat too heavily. Consume broths, vegetable juices, and often easily assimilated foods. Get vitamin B and B complex from celery, lettuce, carrots, tomatoes, pears, berries, and Fleischmann's yeast.

Olive Oil: Use small amounts two to three times daily for seven to ten days, rest, then repeat.

Sample Diet

BREAKFAST

Stewed prunes
Corn meal
Milk or Saffron

MIDMORNING

Citrus fruit
Olive oil

LUNCH

Green leafy salad (lettuce, celery, mustard greens, spinach)
Ground soaked almonds or almond butter with honey on rye bread
Dish of pears
Drink of slippery elm water

SUPPER

Wild game or broiled fish
Eggplant, green beans, leaf lettuce salad with safflower oil dressing
Baked yam
Dish of baked apples
Cup of tea or coffee
Spoonful of beef juice in afternoon and evening

3. Asthma

The elements of a good diet for the asthmatic are: (1) severe restriction of sweets (honey allowed only once a day); (2) no white bread, potatoes,

tomatoes, dried beans, or rice; (3) all fruits, vegetables, and nuts generally are desirable; (4) fowl or
fish are preferable for protein.

Avoid: Sweets, starches, stimulants, tea
or coffee, rutabaga, and red meats.

Fruits: Citrus fruit; prunes, prune whip,
or prune juice for the eliminations;
and rhubarb.

Vegetables: Pokeweed (boil and make a tea), all
forms of leafy green vegetables (raw
and cooked), dock (for cleansing
and purification), red cabbage,
spinach, carrots, celery, lettuce
(any of these in gelatin), onions,
radishes, and parsnips.

Protein: Chicken, fresh fish, lamb's tongue,
and eggs and milk in moderation
if can be tolerated (soy milk can be
used as a substitute).

Grains: Whole wheat grains and rye.

Supplements: Calcios (for bone building) and
beef juices, specially prepared.
(Calcios is available from the Heri-
tage Store, Virginia Beach, VA and
Cayce Corner, 4018 N. 40th Street,
Phoenix, AZ, 85018).

          The body needs more of an al-
kaline diet (the sugars tend to

make acid). Therefore the fruit
juices and vegetable juices are better than soft drinks or alcohol.
Watch eliminations—cleansing is
necessary.

4. Cardiovascular Disease

Basically, nearly all cardiovascular problems
have the same nutritional and dietary deficiencies
and need very similar correctional dietary measures.

The diet is a major element in treatment. In
arteriosclerosis, for instance, one should use little
starch or sugar; lots of vitamin B-1 (found in the
yellow foods like corn, squash, carrots, oranges,
and lemons); no red meats (fish, fowl, or lamb are
instead suggested); lots of green foods to create an
alkaline-reacting diet; well-balanced meals, such
as shown in the A.R.E. Clinic's Basic Diet. (Found
in Chapter 5.)

Certain general factors always seem to surface, and should be given attention, no matter
which part of the cardiovascular system is hurt-
ing.

In the diet—not too great quantities of
foods, but those that are easily assimilated; and feed the body rather three to
four to five times each day, than just the
regular periods—but small quantities.

1241-1

The diet should be not of meats so much; though fowl or lamb may be taken in moderation, but no red meats at any time, no white bread. The vegetables should be more of those as above the ground than those below.

1275–1

For a man who was diagnosed as having had a very recent coronary thrombosis:

In the diets—those foods that are easily assimilated. We find that occasionally the Jerusalem artichoke would be most helpful, EASING those tendencies in the liver and pancreas area for the formations of sugars there, that tend to produce [cirrhosis] that hardness that becomes a part of the disturbance—in the liver area.

1767–3

And, for a woman who had had a stroke, the suggestions covered the sort of diet that would be most helpful for strengthening the body as recovery progressed:

In the manner of the diets, necessary—as we find—that there be considered that there should be more strengthening food, yet keep the feeding not too much but rather the more often.

As we find, such as a coddled egg with toast as the morning meal; alternated at times with whole wheat cereal or with fruit juices, though do not have the ce-

reals *and* the citrus fruits at the same
meal—or even on the same day. If one is
taken one day, take the other the next.
Fruit juices may be taken in the afternoon
of the same day, as pineapple juice or the
like. But oranges, lemons, grapefruit—do
not take these with cereals or on the same
day; let at least there be four to eight
hours difference between their taking. For
to take those that are acid and alkaline
reacting, and to take any food values as of
cereals with the citrus fruit juices, defeats
the purpose and creates an acid-producing reaction in the system that's not good.

Vegetable juices, and a little of the
vegetables. Fowl, if it is well cooked *as*
broth—or the broth of same with the meat
well cooked as with noodles or the like.

Have more of the starches, but keep a
balance between same and the proteins as
would be with those of such meats with
same, see?

Fruit juices, vegetable juices in between; beef juice itself *well prepared*, no
fat in same, this sipped occasionally, with
a Graham Cracker. Have this well seasoned with salt; not too saline, to be sure,
but these are necessary for the creating of
blood supply—not as to overtax, but to
supply the elements, the nutriments that
will create the plasm in the bloodstream
that makes more perfect coagulation.

1187–7

122

5. Colitis

Chronic mucous colitis—sometimes called spastic colitis or occasionally ulcerative colitis—in the older person is approached somewhat differently from that which might be found in the child.

With the adult, the readings sometimes recommended tuberous vegetables, at other times suggested a "regular" diet, and at times a diet as found in the following reading:

> In the diets, keep away from meats. Only fish and fowl may be taken, and these never fried. *No fried foods of any kind.* Take rather the bodybuilding and strength-giving foods—especially a great deal of fruits, fruit juices—including citrus fruit juices, of course. Combine a little lemon with the orange juice. Plenty of prunes, prune whip. Plenty of pineapple and the like. All of these would be the principles, though not all of the diet. Refrain from a great deal of pastries. Malted milks and those of such natures may be in the diet. Not too much of candies or sweets, though occasionally milk in chocolate or cocoa and the like may be taken.
>
> 2085–1

In the child, the procedure was underfeeding—at least in the case of a six-and-a-half-year-old boy (3886). He was given vegetable and citrus fruit juices and goat's milk. In addition to rest and quiet, he was also given beef juice for strengthening the body. A child will need more starches when healthy because of the normal high level of a child's activity. When ill, however, the limitation of sugars and starches is necessary, thus the under-feeding Cayce suggested.

6. Cystitis

The matter of diet relates primarily to the acid-alkaline balance of the system. In most cases of cystitis the system has a tendency to be overly acidic. Hence, the diet is generally alkaline in nature:

> . . . As to the diets—these are very well if kept in a balance of at least eighty percent alkaline-producing to twenty percent of the acid-producing. This would then indicate not great quantities of sugars or of sweets, though honey may be taken. But beware of cakes or icing or great quantities of sugar or candy. Honey, especially with the honeycomb, may be taken as the sweets. Not a great quantity, ever of course of fried foods. Not great quantities ever of white bread, but rather use rye or whole wheat or the like—these are the more preferable. . . .
>
> 540–11

> As to the diet—after the period of the cleansing of the alimentary canal, and making for the activity of the liver, the spleen, the kidneys, as to their general

activity—there should not be a great deal of meat. Never any hog meat, except occasionally a little crisp bacon may be taken. Fish, fowl, and lamb should be the meats, and these not every day—and never fried.

Leafy vegetables are preferable to the tuberous or bulbous nature. A raw salad should be one meal each day, or at least part of same. Include raw carrots, lettuce, celery, watercress, and especially beet tops. These may all be taken raw, if properly prepared. For this particular body, these would be better in bulk than just taking the juices of same; though for some bodies the juices would be better.

As for breads—only corn bread, using the yellow meal, with egg, and whole wheat bread. These are preferable.

3050–1

A method for obtaining a rough idea of the acidity or alkalinity of the system is given in one of the readings:

. . . A general activity for a body in much of a normal condition is to keep the acidity and the alkalinity in a proper balance. The best manner to indicate this is to test the alkalinity or acidity of the body through the salivary glands or through the salivary gland membranes, or by taking the litmus paper in the mouth. This also may be indicated through the urine.

Whenever there is disturbance with

this, if it is in the glands themselves, then take citrocarbonate—that is, if it is indicated in the salivary glands that there is an acidity, then take a small quantity of citrocarbonate. If the acidity is indicated through the kidneys, or from the urine itself, then drink a little of the carbonated waters, as would be indicated with Coca-Cola—but that which is BOTTLED is the better; OR use a little of the watermelon seed tea. Either of these would tend to make for a balance.

520–11

7. Diabetes

Diet is highly important. Cayce indicated that "in diabetic tendencies the diet has more to do with the reactions obtained than most any other application . . ." (3086–1). Jerusalem artichokes are suggested in every case of diabetes. These provide a type of pseudo-insulin material for the body, which helps restore normal function of the pancreas. They should be eaten in varying amounts three times a week or, if the case is more severe, one a day for five to six days a week. They should be cooked—one artichoke about the size of a hen's egg—in Patapar paper, prepared with the juices, and eaten in that manner. If they are taken five or six days a week they should be used raw one day and cooked the next. In reading 1878–1, Cayce says, "for taking the artichoke—especially this Jerusalem variety—is using insulin but in a manner that is *not* habit forming, and is much more preferable—if it is governed properly—with the rest of the diet."

The Jerusalem artichoke or *Helianthus tuberosus*, also called the girasole, is unique in that it stores its carbohydrates as inulin or inulides (which yields levulose, or fructose, or hydrolysis) rather than as starch (which yields glucose). The levulose is not as harmful to the body in diabetes as glucose is. Medical opinion has been divided on its use. For the sake of reference, I will note that insulin is a protein hormone, a plant-derived fructose polysaccharide, while glucokinin is a hormonelike substance that is obtained from plants and that will produce hypoglycemia in animals and will act on depancreatized dogs in a manner similar to insulin. Some plants contain glucokinin, but apparently this has not been found yet in the Jerusalem artichoke.

Otherwise in the diet, it should be advised that one eat no red meats, little meat of any kind, minimal sweets, less starch, no white sugar, no white bread. The various kinds of pastries and pies, should be avoided. Coffee or tea should not be taken more than once daily. Fish or fowl should be eaten in small amounts. There should be many leafy vegetables in the diet; very little of the pod variety; and no vegetables grown below ground, with the exception of oyster plant, carrots, or beets occasionally (and the beet should be taken with the beet top). No fried foods should be eaten.

Sample Menu

BREAKFAST

Coddled egg
Corn muffins
Dish of fresh blueberries or baked apple
Health tea—Sassafras

LUNCH

Fresh leafy vegetable salad (spinach, endive, leaf
lettuce, carrots, with unsaturated oil dressing)
Bowl of barley soup
Glass of Bulgarian buttermilk

SUPPER

Steamed beets and tops
Sliced tomatoes
Baked fish
Asparagus/Jerusalem artichoke
Dish of peaches
Coffee

8. Epilepsy

The diet for epilepsy should generally contain
foods of a nonconstipating and easily digestible
nature. Overeating should be avoided.

1. *Sugars and starches:* Use honey for sweetening. Cut down on starches. Avoid sugars
   and condiments.
2. *Fruits:* All in abundance except raw apples,

bananas, large prunes, plums, and cran-berries.
3. *Vegetables:* Especially stress raw, green vegetable salads. Eat leafy vegetables in abundance rather than tuberous vegetables (except carrots, beets, and oyster plant). Avoid potatoes, turnips, legumes, and rhubarb. Eat Jerusalem artichokes one or two times a week, and okra frequently.
4. *Cereal products:* Whole wheat, cracked wheat, or pumpernickel bread. Eat dry cereals, whole wheat or steel-cut oats (not rolled oats) as cooked cereals, but not at the same meal with citrus fruits. No nuts, except filberts and almonds in moderation. Ovaltine is good as a beverage, rather than coffee or tea.
5. *Meats:* Seafoods in abundance but never fried. Fish, fowl, lamb, calve's liver (broiled, never fried), no rare meat, no beef except beef juice regularly, no fat meats, no pork except crisp breakfast bacon occasionally. Use gelatin frequently (e.g., in fruit and vegetable salads).
6. *Dairy products:* Eggs, but only the yolk. Cheese only in moderation. Avoid sweet milk (use Bulgarian buttermilk, dry skimmed milk, or soybean milk).
7. *Miscellaneous:* No carbonated beverages. No alcoholic drinks. No smoking unless already an addict, then decrease to a minimum. Ovaltine is better than coffee or tea.

9. Hypoglycemia

Upon arising	Medium orange, half a grapefruit, or four ounces of fresh or unsweetened juice.
BREAKFAST	Fruit or unsweetened juice. One egg with or without two slices of crisp bacon. One slice of whole wheat or rye bread or toast with butter. Beverage.
Midmorning	Medium size fruit with a glass of milk.
LUNCH	Moderate amount of meat, fish, cheese, or fowl. Salad (large serving of leafy green vegetables and tomato) with mayonnaise or oil dressing. One slice of whole wheat or rye bread with butter. Dessert and beverage.
Early afternoon	Glass of milk (eight ounces). Cheese or nuts.
Late afternoon	Fresh or unsweetened fruit juice (four ounces).
DINNER	Soup if desired. Liberal portion of lamb, fish, or fowl. Vegetables. One slice of bread if desired. Dessert. Beverage.
Two to three hours after	Glass of milk (eight ounces).

Every two hours
  until bedtime   Small glass of milk (four
ounces) or handful of nuts or
cheese.

Allowed

Vegetables: Asparagus, avocado, beets, broccoli, brussels sprouts, cabbage, cauliflower, carrots, celery, corn, cucumber, eggplant, lima beans, onions, peas, radishes, sauerkraut, string beans, tomatoes, and turnips.

Fruits: Apples, apricots, berries, grapefruit, melon, oranges, peaches, pears, pineapple, and tangerines. These may be cooked or raw, with or without cream, but without sugar. Canned fruits should be packed in water. Avoid dried fruits such as dates, raisins, and apricots because of high sugar content. Large amounts of any fruit may contain too much sugar for you.

Beverages: Weak tea and decaffeinated coffee or substitutes. May be sweetened with saccharin or sucaryl. Any unsweetened fruit or vegetable juice, except grape or prune juice.

Desserts and miscellaneous: Fruit, unsweetened gelatin, junket (made from tablet, not mix), and yogurt. Lettuce, mushrooms, or nuts may be taken as freely as desired.

Prohibited

All alcoholic and soft drinks: This includes club soda. Alcoholic beverages usually have a high carbohydrate content.

Sugar, candy, and other sweets: Cakes, pie, pastries, pudding, ice cream, and honey.

Caffeine: Coffee, strong brewed tea, or any other beverage containing caffeine.

To Be Avoided
(Use Only Rarely)

Starchy foods: Potatoes, rice, bananas, spaghetti, noodles, doughnuts, and white bread.

Foods high in sugar: Grapes, raisins, figs, dates, jams, jellies, and plums.

Pork: Except crisp bacon.

Large meals: Frequent small meals of a high protein, low carbohydrate diet help maintain your blood sugar at a normal level that eliminates the unpleasant effects of hypoglycemia.

10. Migraine Headaches

Two of the readings Edgar Cayce gave about the problem of migraine headaches dealt to a great extent with diet. His suggestions are a bit unusual, but he gives a diet program that may be helpful in most instances of migraine:

> In the manner of the diet: Beware of ANY character of food that even creates a great quantity of alcohol, or of ANY alcohol, . . . Those drinks with a little charged water would be very well—as Coca-Cola or Orangeade or the like, if

taken once or twice a day; for their reaction upon the system as related to especially the hepatic or the kidney AND liver circulation would be good.

Beware of starches or combinations of starches that produce the excesses.

Let this be rather as an outline, though not JUST these foods taken—but foods of these natures:

Mornings—citrus fruit juices, or whole wheat cereals—as Maltex or Crushed Wheat, that are well, WELL cooked (but do not combine cereals AND citrus fruits at the same meal!). These may be altered at times also with stewed fruits; as figs, the pie plant, or tomato juice . . . all of these should be taken at one time or another. Coffee may be taken if it is desired, with brown toast at the meal—but WITHOUT cream or milk in same!

Noons—preferably have as a portion of same only raw vegetables combined together. Vegetable juices may be taken at this time. The shellfish may be taken at this time, in their various forms.

Evenings—only the vegetables and meats that are well cooked and well balanced. No fried foods at any time. The meats should consist principally of fish, fowl, or lamb. Have three vegetables above the ground to one below the ground.

1476-2

Here, with this body, it would require sufficient colonic irrigations, scientifically given, to keep the colon cleansed for a period sufficient for reaction of the body energies themselves in supplying nutriment to the folds in the colon itself.

This extends and becomes much more active in the jejunum (this is speaking universally now, not in this individual case) but its beginnings are in the area (as in this particular body) of the cecum—where the jejunum empties into the colon for further digestions and absorption by body forces.

Hence with this body, to be sure, throughout these periods keep away from excesses of sweets, especially chocolate and any sedimentary forces (such as brans or as raisins). Prunes will work just the opposite, for these carry another form of activity to the walls of the system itself. It would be well to include prunes in the diet, if they are cooked—or even fresh. Plums of all natures, then, are very well to be taken.

Certain forms of apples are well, but most of these for this body through these periods should be cooked.

Water Cress, especially, should be taken—and these raw; including celery and lettuce; at times carrots. All of these grated and combined with the gelatin would be much better for the body.

Do drink plenty of water, at least six to eight glasses of water each day.

Do have sufficient enemas, scientifically given, to cleanse all mucus from the
body. This may be done each time the
colonic is given. So put them about ten
days to two weeks apart, and there should
be required at least four or five of these.

During that same period, relax the
body osteopathically; with special reference to reducing a lesion that exists between the 6th and 7th dorsal.

Do these, being mindful of the diet,
and we will correct conditions for this
body. These are the sources of migraine
headaches.

3326–1

11. Obesity

It is true that all cases of obesity cannot be
controlled by diet alone. Any physician working
with problems of obesity has found this to be a
very troublesome fact. Yet diet is always a portion
of the therapy and sometimes will do the job completely. The following Cayce suggestions give one
approach toward helping keep weight under con-
trol in the human body. There are, of course,
unconscious habit patterns that hinder the effort,
and emotional/glandular difficulties that likewise
keep people from achieving success in reducing
weight. The use of diluted grape juice, however,
has been a very helpful method of using diet to
reduce body weight:

As we find, to prevent the excesses of
weight for this body, we would use also

135

the grape juice. This three-fourths grape juice to one-fourth water, or a small glass of four ounces four times a day. This taken before meals and before retiring. Unless this becomes to the body as heavy upon the system, it will be found to prove beneficial to eliminations, and prevent the use of or desire for starches or sweets; and will give the inclination for the body to keep a normal balance in weight. The Welch's as we find is the preferable for this, when the fresh grapes are not available.

470–19

. . . Beware that the body does not become overweight. This might, of course, become an aggravating condition to the body. Use grape juice about four times a day, at least four days of the week; one ounce of grape juice (Welch's, preferably) in one and one-half ounces of plain water (not carbonated), about thirty minutes before each meal and before retiring at night. This will keep down too much sugar, and will aid better in the eliminations through the kidneys.

2514–11

As to the increase in weight—this may be controlled by the grape juice way, rather than any particular dieting; just requiring that the body refrain from too much sweets and starches.

470–32

Q-2: Should starches and sweets be eliminated from the diet or to what extent may they be eaten?

A-2: As indicated, if the grape juice is taken it supplies a sugar, the kind of sugar though that works with the system—that which is necessary, see? And then that prevents the system's desire for starches and sweets in excess. Not that these are not to be taken at all, for they supply, of course, the necessary heat units for the body in a great measure; but as these would be supplied through the taking of the grape juice, or the eating of the grapes (if they are taken AS the regular diet, and not just occasionally), there would only be the partaking of others as the appetite calls for same. When the appetite is controlled, it will govern the necessary forces in these directions.

470–19

Q-6: Please outline a reducing diet.

A-6: Eat anything you like, save potatoes and white bread. But take four glasses of Welch's Grape Juice each day—half an hour before the meals and before retiring. This would be three-quarters of a glass of the grape juice and one-quarter of plain water stirred together. Take about five to ten minutes to drink the juice each time, see?

1431–2

12. Psoriasis

Treatment of psoriasis is threefold in purpose: to restore balance and coordination between the various organs of assimilation and elimination; to clear the circulatory and alimentary systems of the accumulated toxic substances; and to promote healing of the intestinal lesions that allow the toxic substances to leak into the circulatory system.

The utmost importance must be placed on proper diet, since this aids substantially in accomplishing all three desired objectives. The diet, of course, will vary somewhat from case to case but generally emphasizes fresh fruits and raw and cooked vegetables with no meat other than fish, fowl, and lamb:

> . . . stress seafoods and fowl. Little of beef or other meats. Use at least three vegetables that grow above the ground to one that grows under the ground, and we will find better conditions for this body.

> 3373–1

> Eliminate fats, sweets, and pastries from the diet. Do have a great deal of fruits and vegetables. . . .

> 5016–1

Q-2: *Can the body take any kind of alcoholic beverages?*
A-2: Wines; but not the stronger drinks—not rum or the like.

> 745–1

In nearly every case improvement in diet is one of the first treatments instituted. Since toxic accumulations in the circulation and tissues tends to be acid in nature, the general character of the improved diet is such as to promote alkalinity and thus bring about a better acid-alkaline balance to the entire system. The diet is much more specific in some cases than in others, but in all cases it tends to be alkaline in content. It also emphasizes fresh fruits and vegetables to promote better eliminations through the intestinal tract:

> In the diet we would keep rather to the non-acid foods; that is, keeping rather the alkaline-reacting foods; letting one meal each day consist of raw vegetables wholly. With such there may be used an oil or salad dressing.
>
> 745–1

Diet

1. No carbonated water.
2. No meat other than fish, fowl, and lamb.
3. Eliminate fats, sweets, pastries.
4. Wine is permitted, but no other alcohol.
5. Emphasize yellow-colored foods such as corn meal, carrots, and peaches. Peaches should be the only sweets eaten. Grape juice is also good.

SUGGESTED BREAKFAST

Three mornings a week: Cereal consisting of rolled, crushed, or cracked whole wheat. Do not overcook.

On other mornings: Citrus fruit or juices, yolks of soft-boiled or poached eggs, whole wheat toast with butter.

Beverage: milk or black coffee. Occasionally breakfast may consist of a baked apple wih cream or stewed prunes or apricots or figs. Do not eat citrus fruit and cereal at the same meal.

LUNCH

Salad consisting entirely of fresh raw vegetables. Include tomatoes, lettuce, celery, spinach, beet tops, mustard, onions, or similar produce (except cucumbers). Salad oil or dressing permitted. Make the salad do for the entire meal.

EVENING

Small cup of soup or broth. Cooked vegetables should make up the major portion of the meal. There may be small portions of lamb, fish, or fowl. No fried foods should be eaten.

TEAS

Yellow saffron (sometimes called American saffron, or saffron). Drink one cup each evening at bedtime. Place the tea (start with a pinch) in a cup of boiling water and allow to steep for about twenty to thirty minutes. Use more tea if preferred.

Mullein tea may be taken on alternate days. Use one teaspoon of mullein to a pint of boiling water. Steep for thirty minutes, strain, cool, and drink within three or four hours.

13. Scleroderma

The diet recommended for scleroderma is an alkaline-forming one with many leafy vegetables as the main portion. Fish, fowl, and lamb are all right, but fried foods should never be used. Vegetable soups and other foods easily assimilated are recommended, vegetables cooked with Patapar paper or the equivalent parchment paper that may be purchased in most health food stores. Meat should not be cooked with the vegetable soups.

The following lists those things that should be considered as far as diet is concerned:

1. Beef juice is considered a medication.
2. Red wine with black bread or Ry Krisp for an afternoon or evening snack, if desired.
3. Plenty of orange juice and other citrus fruit juices.
4. Liver, pig's feet, and tripe.
5. Lots of vegetables: carrots and gelatin, beets and gelatin, watercress, celery, lettuce, tomatoes.
6. Vegetable soups without meats or fats.
7. Use Patapar paper to cook vegetables in.

Next in line are the Don'ts regarding your diet:

1. Eat very few starches. They can be harmful to the body.
2. Don't combine citrus with cereals at the same meal, or even in the same day.

3. Don't eat anything that has been pickled.
4. Don't eat too many:
    a. Heavy or hard-to-digest foods.
    b. Meats or nuts.
5. Don't eat any beef, pork, or fried foods.

CANCER DIETARY SUGGESTIONS

What part should diet play in the care of those who have cancer? Does nutrition and the acceptance of foods in the intestinal tract really have anything to do with the recovery of an individual who has developed cancer?

This topic is still being hotly debated. It is agreed that eating a high-roughage diet will prevent a certain number of cancers of the colon. Roughage is defined as green vegetables, bran, and certain fruits containing a high proportion of indigestible cellulose, stimulates peristalsis in the intestines.

Such a diet is alkaline-reacting and parallels the suggestions found in the Cayce readings for nearly all those who have cancer of any kind. A highly alkaline-reacting diet is the basis of health in these readings and throughout my experience as a physician.

Cancer of the human body can never be healed by diet alone. I say this guardedly, for I have known instances where this apparently has happened. However, throughout this book the need for changes other than diet has been emphasized, and the best diet in the world without belief in that diet will generally accomplish nothing in *any* illness. It would be foolhardy to use only a dietary regimen when a person is afflicted with cancer and expect that alone to bring about a cure.

No matter what kind of a cancer is found to be active in the body, however, a well thought out diet that is usually preventative and alkaline-reacting in nature can aid the healing effort that has already been instituted by the family physician, the internist, the surgeon, or the oncologist. Sometimes the diet has to be bodybuilding because of severe weight loss. All factors need attention when dealing with a life-threatening situation.

Perhaps the best way to describe some of the dietary ideas in the readings that may be helpful in the treatment of specific types of cancer is to quote several of the readings. No comprehensive treatment program can be derived out of this material without much study of all the suggestions and an adequate amount of clinical work—which hasn't really been done up to the present time:

> In the matter of the diets, the body finds—and will find more and more— these have much to do with the general reaction in the system, and that a general alkaline in the system is the more satisfactory reaction; less and less of greases of any nature are the better conditions and are more easily assimilated, and the reactions of those properties in the system for the creating of better coagulation through the body are the better.

> 325—42

We may add such elements in the diet as to be helpful, but not curative.

As we find, these will add to the ability of the bloodstream to resist, or to build coagulations:

Take about twice daily a drink made with milk, egg, and a very small quantity of whiskey; just enough whiskey to cook the yolk of the egg—or a teaspoonful poured on the yolk, and then all of the white beaten in it; then this stirred in about half to three-quarters of a glass of milk.

About two, three, or four times a week, it will be helpful to take either the liver or oxblood pudding. Either or both of these will make for helpful forces, though not curative forces. Use as much blood in same as practical, though cook to some extent.

2918–1

Beware in the diet of any highly seasoned foods, or too much of those of certain bulbous natures; as beans (that are dried), as the white potato.

However, those of the bulbous nature such as the artichoke (any form; there are three that are edible) or the oyster plant are beneficial; also those that carry more of that dextrin of the better nature for any inflammatory conditions.

Also those foods that are purifying and cleansing in nature would be well; such as the GREENS (the tops, of course, not the roots); as mustard, lambs' tongue, poke (not pork meat, but poke greens [pokeweed]) and their combinations.

Not too much of turnips—either the greens or the bulbous part; but those other greens which carry HEALING and cleansing forces are well.

601–27

To a woman who had a sarcoma, asking for help in the very late stages, Cayce had several things to say. He told her it was a karmic thing: "We do something to start this and then we meet it in the circulation." He also told her that the things he was suggesting were not curative. But he did offer help:

These will bring ease. These will not cure, but are sources of help—and if studied—the juices of the Plantain weed and the keeping away from certain food values—help may be brought even to many individuals suffering with the same.

3387–1

Feed *all* the food that is of a *nourishing* nature, but not from *meats*. Those of cereals, fruits, vegetables, *and* such—or principally of the nature that are the foods of the hare, the foods of the beef—these are *destructive* forces *to* such as may be seen in the condition attacking system.

2457–4

145

Q-3: Why do foods not agree with him?
A-3: Where there has been those activities that are
using up the digestive foods, or the digestive fluids
in system, the *digestion* is hard to assimilate—
and produces irritation. Those of more of the pre-
digested nature. Instead of milk, there should be
those of the *malted* or the *dried.* These will assimilate better.

5586–2

> In the matter of the diet—have beef
> juice, liver and liver extract, and the whole
> grain cereals as purifiers and in blood
> building; as carrots, beets especially and
> beet tops. These should be portions of the
> diet often. Change these as to their prep-
> aration, so as not to weary the body with
> the same diet, or change in the manner in
> which they would be prepared, and with
> other vegetables.

2956–1

Dealing with the problem of skin cancer,
Cayce includes the instructions on how to prepare
a tea that acts to purify those cells that have gone
astray:

> But to purify these from the body-
> force, we would also take internally a Plan-
> tain Tea, made from the tender top leaves
> of the same plant, with—at this season,
> especially—the seed of the Plantain—
> about half and half. Fill half a pint cup
> with these, and add to one quart of Dis-
> tilled or Rain Water—using only an

enamel or glass container, not metal. Cook until reduced to about half the quantity, or half a pint of the liquid. Take this as a tea, a teaspoonful four times each day; after each meal and at bedtime. Keep this where it is cool, and if the quantity tends to turn a bit sour, discard it—but this whole quantity should be taken before it would sour. It is not so good to add a preservative for this particular material, for it changes this.

In the diet—do live mostly, for a while, on watermelon, carrots, beets; having these almost daily. The watermelon is for the activity of the liver and kidney, the beets and carrots are for the purifying of the blood, as combined with the Plantain Tea and Ointment.

Most of all, pray. Let the mental attitude be considered first and foremost. Do not promise thyself, not thy God, nor thy neighbor, that you do not fulfill.

3121-1

Here is a reading that is applicable to all of these suggestions about diet, in that it leads us to a higher thought, and lets us remember that the diet is important. But attitudes *must* always be considered and utilized in a constructive manner:

Do not make the applications merely as a routine—either the rubs, the diets, or the Appliance. Let these be done with the continuous spiritual purpose to be healed of the disturbances FOR a definite purpose, that is to be constructive and helpful to others; to those about self and to others.

Keep optimistic. Pray often; seeing, feeling, asking, desiring, expecting help— from Him; who is the way, the truth, the light. He faileth not those who keep His purposes.

2514–1

7

---- ※ ----

Commonsense Odds
and Ends

TESTING FOR ALKALINITY

About the time you arrive at the point where you think you have figured out how Cayce understood things in the dietary realm, the picture becomes obscure once again. It may simply be that there is a place for every substance God created in this earth to do good, if used in the proper manner.

For example, some say that any form of alcohol is bad—that you should never use it. Yet Jesus changed water to wine, and it was the best wine at the wedding party. Cayce suggested often that wine—with black bread, in the middle of the afternoon—is a food that is beneficial for the body and builds up the blood. So it has to be good.

Also, in certain areas of the small intestine, foods of certain characters are changed to alcohol; for the body indeed does need alcohol in certain amounts and to use in certain ways. Yet Cayce cautions some that if they are really desirous of longevity, they need to look to the purpose for which they drink alcohol in social situations.

Alcohol, sugars, starches, fats, and proteins all create an acid reaction inside the functioning physical body. There is a health-producing reserve of alkaline in the body, and if that reserve is depleted by too many acids, the body is subject to a variety of diseases. There is an acidosis of the body caused by diabetes, for instance, when the lack of sugar metabolism causes fats to be burned incompletely. Normally, in the healthy individual, acidosis or an increase in body acids comes about when certain foods are "burned" and leave an acid ash.

Food is a fuel, and when metabolized within the body, it leaves a residue that is either acid or alkaline. This is the basis for understanding the acid-alkaline balance. Usually the ratio within the body is four parts alkaline to one part acid. It is difficult to create an alkalosis simply by eating too many foods of an alkaline nature. Acidosis of a nutritional origin is much easier to create—simply eat a preponderance of sugars, starches, meats, gravies and the like and the body will neutralize some of its alkaline reserve and will become over-acid in nature losing much of its normal immune-system-based resistance.

Arthur Snyder has suggested, in his booklet *Foods that Preserve the Alkaline Reserve*, that health depends on the maintainance of a 4:1 ratio in alkaline to acid ash. When the ratio drops to 3:1, health is seriously menaced. His ideas are like those found in the Cayce readings. It becomes important to determine as nearly as possible what state the body is in relative to this balance. How do we test for acidity?

The following three references from the readings give us much clarity, especially if we remember that today Nitrazine paper is much easier to buy than litmus, and is more exact and informational to use for testing the pH of either the sputum or the urine. The Nitrazine paper is simply either dipped into the urine or made wet with the sputum, then the strip is compared to the color shown on the container. The limits are from pH 4.5, which is very yellow and acid, up to 7.5, which is blue and very alkaline. Balance is found at pH 6.0. By testing the sputum and the urine, you can gain some insight into how your body is responding to foods and activity, emotional patterns, stresses, and life situations. While the sputum and the urine can be tested, always remember that this is not the entire body, so an indication may be obtained of the level of alkalinity in the body, but not an exact analysis.

You'll also find, in these readings, how Coca-Cola and citrocarbonate are used in a very interesting and beneficial way for the human body:

Q-6: What diet should be taken?
A-6: There might be one diet given today and then next week you would have another! That which keeps the spittle or salivary reaction alkaline. That which keeps the blood reaction, by test, negative. That which keeps the urine eliminations as a balance at twenty-four (24) without albumin, without sediment, and with an alkaline tendence;

but not too great a tendency. That which makes for the proper eliminations and bodybuilding without becoming superfluous flesh, or drainage to same—see? Hence these are to be kept by *constructive* measures and forces, see?

681–2

As to the matter of diet, be mindful that the food values are kept rather in an alkalin-reacting state; or that the test of litmus paper—both for the spittle and for the urine—show an alkaline reaction, see? This should be maintained more by the diet than by other efforts, you see . . .

593–1

Q-6: Please give some general rules that will help this body to keep in a healthier condition.
A-6: The conditions have arisen, as we have indicated in the first information for these bodies—or at the time of pregnancy, from the lack of precautions at the time of the delivery of the child—as to the kidneys.

When these conditions are cleared up, the body should be in a very good condition to keep in a normal force, with general rules as to health.

A general activity for a body in much of a normal condition is to keep the acidity and the alkalinity in a proper balance. The best manner to indicate this is to test the alkalinity or acidity of the body through the salivary glands or through the salivary gland membranes, or by taking the litmus paper in the mouth. This also may be indicated through the urine.

Whenever there is disturbance with this, if it is in the glands themselves, then take citrocarbonate—that is, if it is indicated in the salivary glands that there is an acidity, then take a small quantity of citrocarbonate. If the acidity is indicated through the kidneys, or from the urine itself, then drink a little of the carbonated waters, as would be indicated with Coca-Cola—but that which is BOTTLED is the better; OR use a little of the Watermelon Seed Tea. Either of these would then to make for a balance.

Then if the proper balance is kept in the diet as indicated—twenty percent acid-producing to eighty percent alkaline-producing—as the conditions are for this body, its age, its temperament and the like—we should keep near normal.

540–11

It's evident at this point that one of the rules in establishing or maintaining health is to keep to the 80:20 alkaline-acid ratio in your diet. And, if you have any doubts, check it!

The place to get this whole procedure off and running, of course, is in your own kitchen. You may have to break long standing habits in order to get this accomplished, but change is what the world is all about. And, like the wheat bowing to the wind, if your ideal leads you to be flexible and always seeking for the twists and turns in the path, you'll have no difficulty.

YOUR NEW-AGE KITCHEN

Once the decision has been made to switch to a more beautiful way of living and eating, we often discover that we must not only change our habits and life-styles, but we must also learn new skills in order to bring these resolutions to life.

The following information gives some practical guidance to all who wish to change and make the decision to create your own New-Age Kitchen. It certainly is not *all* that is needed, but it will get you started.

Suggested Equipment	*Suggested Foods*
Blender	Fresh vegetables and fruit
Sprouter	Sugarless cereals
Juicer (optional)	Honey
Pots for steaming	Raw milk
Steamer basket	Whole grain breads (read labels!)
Stainless steel pots	Whole wheat flour, rye flour
Corning Ware	Fertile eggs
Crockpot	Cheese (farmer's cheese, raw milk cheese)
Tupperware	
Flour mill	
Backyard garden	Yogurt (plain)
Oven	Apple cider vinegar
Refrigerator	Olive oil, peanut oil
NO MICROWAVE OVENS	Nuts
	Garlic
	Sea salt
	Herb teas

Dried beans and lentils
Dried fruits
NO PROCESSED
    FOODS

Cooking and Preparing Foods

Avoid microwave ovens.

Use low temperatures over a long period of time to save time and energy (i.e., put dinner in the crockpot before you leave for work).

Build your own recipe file—it can be a gold mine of information.

Casseroles are great timesavers. You can cook enough beans and rice at one time on a weekend to last the whole week; use them in casseroles as needed.

Chop vegetables for salads ahead of time—say, over a weekend—and keep in a crisper for the rest of the week (ready-to-eat munchables—yogurt and Hidden Valley seasoning make a great dip).

Steam vegetables until still slightly crisp—don't overcook.

Use exotic ingredients in salads for variety—nuts, raisins, apples, plus the whole lineup of vegetables.

Grow as much of your own food as possible.

Use scraps as compost for your backyard garden.

SOURCES OF BASIC NUTRIENTS

One of the most puzzling questions that arise in the course of reworking your diet is which foods supply specific basic nutrients—zinc, for instance—for our bodies. Lots of other similar questions usually lead more deeply into the study of nutrition.

Your own experience will give you beginning answers, for experience is always the best teacher. You might research medical textbooks on nutrition for some of the answers if you wish to delve deeply into the subject. Otherwise there is a variety of sources in diet-oriented books on the market that will give you more information.

My experience through forty years in the practice of medicine has given me much in the way of assistance of unraveling some of these puzzles. And I did get some aid in my medical school education.

Zinc, for instance, is found in beef, eggs, liver, herring, oyster, barley, brown rice, oatmeal, sunflower seeds, kelp and other seaweeds, carrots, and peas.

Complex carbohydrates, which have been discussed so extensively in the media, can always be found in fruits, vegetables of all kinds, and whole grain products.

Vitamin C can be found in profusion in my backyard, for we have oranges and grapefruit growing there. All citrus products are high in vitamin C. Red peppers also give this addition to the diet, as do tomatoes, broccoli, and brussels sprouts.

Vitamin E can be added to the diet in the form of wheat products, especially wheat germ oil. Wheat products should always be whole grain for the best effect. We have helped many apparently sterile women become pregnant simply by increasing the intake of Vitamin E through wheat germ oil capsules.

Vitamin A can be increased through any of the yellow vegetables or fruits, such as apricots, corn, cantaloupe, carrots, or squash. And Vitamin D is probably best found in milk or eggs, especially if the milk is fortified.

Potassium is found in most foods. Excellent sources are cereals, dried peas and beans, fresh vegetables, fresh or dried fruits, fruit juices such as orange or prune, sunflower seeds, watermelon, nuts, molasses, cocoa, fresh fish, beef, and poultry.

Iron is essential to the formation of hemoglobin in the blood, which brings oxygen to all parts of the body. Best sources are almonds, asparagus, bran, beans, cauliflower, celery, chard, Boston brown bread, egg yolk, kidney, liver, oatmeal, oysters, soybeans, and whole wheat. All meats provide iron for the body. Iron is found in a large variety of vegetables, such as cabbage, peppers, cucumbers, peas, prunes, and radishes.

Calcium is most often thought of as pills to be taken. But excellent sources of food calcium are to be found in beans, cauliflower, chard, cheese, cream, egg yolk, kale, milk, molasses, and rhubarb. Some calcium is also found in almonds, beets, bran, cabbage, carrots, celery, chocolate, dates, figs, lemons, lettuce, oranges, oysters, pineapple, raspberries, shellfish, spinach, turnips, walnuts, and watercress.

Magnesium, which helps to build bones and muscle in the body, is found extensively in foods that come to most tables, so it is seldom in deficient supply in the body tissues and bloodstream unless there is a disease process present that prevents its absorption. An ample supply of it is found in fruits, vegetables, and a variety of grains.

Proteins are complex nitrogenous compounds, occurring naturally in plants and animals, which give amino acids when hydrolyzed. Because of the amino acids the proteins contain, proteins are essential for the growth and repair of animal tissue. The best sources are milk, eggs, cheese, meat, fish, and some vegetables such as soybeans. However, proteins are also found in a variety of vegetables, nuts (such as almonds), wheat germ, and brewer's yeast.

Unsaturated fats are thought to be the best kind of fats for the body. Recent research has shown that olive oil and peanut oil—both monounsaturated oils—protect best against arteriosclerosis and are better for consumption than the polyunsaturated oils. But vegetable and most nut oils, salad dressings, and nuts and nut butter are all sources of the unsaturated fats.

As far as other vitamins are concerned—such as thiamin, riboflavin, niacin, folic acid, pantothenic acid, and B-12—these probably are present in your diet if eggs and egg yolk are used, along with fish and fowl, glandular and organ meats (liver, kidneys, and heart), wheat germ products, and leafy green fresh vegetables.

Repeatedly, the information comes from the readings that nature is the best source and that there is a better way to administer these substances than most of us are currently using. That's what proper combinations and the acid-alkaline balance are all about.

Here are two examples of what Cayce had to say about vitamins and minerals that relates to the information just given on nutrients:

> All such properties [as vitamins] that add to the system are more efficacious if they are given for periods, left off for periods and begun again. For if the system comes to rely upon such influences wholly it ceases to produce the vitamins even though the food values may be kept normally balanced.
>
> And it's much better that these be produced in the body from the normal development than supplied mechanically, for nature is much better YET than science!
>
> This we find, then, given twice a day for two or three weeks, left off for a week and then begun again, especially through the winter months, would be much more effective with the body.
>
> 759-12

> These we would keep—not too alkaline in the diet, not too acid, but a well balanced diet. Of mornings, have citrus fruits oft, with hot cakes, eggs, bacon or the like, or alter to cereals—both dry and

cooked; but do not take these the same day that the citrus fruits are taken.

Noons—if practical, either soups, green vegetables or the like.

Evenings—plenty of cooked vegetables, more of the leafy than the pod or tuberous—these are preferable. Fish, fowl, and lamb are preferable for meats, but occasionally a good, thick steak—but cook it WELL. Very seldom have hog meat, though liver, the pigs' feet, the ear, any of those portions that are the digestive foods, that are palatable for the body, are very good—if prepared properly.

. . . As indicated, with the outlines of the diets given we should keep minerals very well balanced.

1467–11

CAYCE TALKS ABOUT FOODS

Cayce's readings frequently pointed up some advice about a specific food, and sometimes he suggested what the food might do for the body as an aid in the healing process. It was for that reason—the illness—that he was consulted.

You might find the following list interesting. It certainly does not explore *all* the foods; this is simply a sampling. But it will give you the flavor of how these readings dealt with the atoms and the molecules that make up any food substance—the energy that is present within each of those things that Cayce discusses. And, you just *may* find something here that will tickle your fancy and say to you, "Hey, this could help *me*!"

1. Alcohol

*Q: Have personal vices as tobacco and whiskey
any influence on one's health or longevity?*
A: As just has been indicated, you are suffering
from the use of some of these in the present; but
it is overindulgence. In moderation these are not
too bad, but man so seldom will be moderate. Or,
as most say, those who even indulge will make
themselves pigs, but we naturally are pigs when
there is overindulgence. This, of course, makes for
conditions which are to be met. For what one sows
that must one reap. This is unchangeable law . . .

5233–1

*Q: Is the moderate use of liquor, tobacco, and
meat a bar to spiritual growth?*
A: For this entity, yes. For some, no.

2981–1

2. Almonds

. . . And know, if ye would take each day,
through thy experience, two almonds, ye
will never have skin blemishes, ye will
never be tempted even in body toward cancer or toward those things that make
blemishes in the body-forces themselves . . .

1206–13

3. Apples—and the Apple Diet

. . . No apples save cooked; these may be
prepared in sauce, or roasted, baked or
the like.

2424–1

It would be well for this body, even after this, to have a three-day apple diet, even in its weakened condition we need to clear the system. For this will get rid of the tendencies for neuritic conditions in the joints of the body. Also take the olive oil after the three-day diet. But don't go without the apples—eat them—all you can—at least five or six apples each day. Chew them up, scrape them well. Drink plenty of water, and follow the three-day diet with the big dose of olive oil.

1409–9

Cayce suggested a dose of olive oil, varying from two or three teaspoonfuls to half a cup. It depends, I'm sure, on the size and vigor of the body—and also on whether or not there is a stone in the gallbladder.

4. Beef Juice

Cayce believed that the body derives several benefits from regular use of beef juice. Apparently it could bring about a strengthening of the body without irritating the cells in the intestinal tract—which might bring about a change in the nature of the lymph and the lymphatic functioning that might in turn disturb the body, causing sleeplessness and general irritation. The following is a commentary on it and a description of how to make beef juice:

. . . The combinations that have been indicated for the body as to diet are very good; yet we would add the greater strengthening influence without the addition of weight or of heavy foods—which would materially aid, and would not irritate those tendencies for the accumulations or separations in the active forces of mucous that has produced and does produce in the lymph those segregations and accumulations about which the body becomes so disturbed at times.

These as we find may be had in the Pure Beef Juice; not broth, but prepared in this manner:

Take a pound to a pound and a half preferably of the round steak, no fat, no portions other than that which is of the muscle or tendon or strength; no fatty or skin portions. Dice this into half-inch cubes, as it were, or practically so. Put same in a glass jar without water in same. Put the jar then into a boiler or container with the water coming about half or three-fourths toward the top of the jar, you see. Preferably put a cloth in the container to prevent the jar from cracking. Do not seal the jar tight, but cover the top. Let this boil (the water, with the jar in same) for three to four hours. Then strain off the juice, and the refuse may be pressed somewhat. It will be found that the meat or flesh itself will be worthless. Place the juice in a cool place, but do not keep too long; never longer than three days, see? Hence the quantity made up at the time depends upon how much or how often the body will take this. It should be taken two to three times a day but not more than a tablespoonful at a time—and this sipped very slowly. Of course, this is to be seasoned to suit the taste of the body.

1343–2

5. Banana and Buttermilk Diet

Q-2: Is the buttermilk and bananas a good eliminating diet?
A-2: The buttermilk and banana diet is very good. . . . The buttermilk and banana diet is rather as a balancing than as an eliminant; for it produces the absorption of certain toxic forces, and the adjustment of other conditions through the system.

538–65

6. Coffee and Tea

Tea is more harmful than coffee. Any nerve reaction is more susceptible to the character of tea that is usually found in this country, though in some manners in which it is produced it would be well. Coffee, taken properly, is a food; that is, *without* cream or milk.

303–2

. . . coffee is as of those properties as stimulants to the nerve system. The dross from same is caffeine, and is not digestible in the system, and must necessarily

then be eliminated. .When such are allowed to remain in the colon there is
thrown off from same poisons. Eliminated
as it is in this system, coffee is a food
value, and is preferable to many stimulants that might be taken, see?

294–86

7. Grape Diet

. . . Some days, for at least three or four
days, eat only GRAPES—Morning, noon,
and night—GRAPES! Not with the seed,
to be sure, but preferably those of the
purple variety; not the larger but those
that are good and NOT those that have
been shipped or kept too long. . . .

1703–1

8. Honey and Milk

Honey and milk should be taken as a
nightcap, as it were. Stir or dissolve a full
teaspoonful of strained honey into a glass
or tumbler of heated milk. Taking this
about twenty to thirty minutes before retiring will be found to be most helpful,
most beneficial.

1539–1

9. Jerusalem Artichokes

Q: What about my cravings for sweets?
A: This is natural with the indigestion and the
lack of proper activity of the pancreas. Eat a Jeru-

salem artichoke once each week, about the size of a hen egg. Cook this in Patapar paper, preserving all the juices to mix with the bulk of the artichoke. Season to taste. This will also aid in the disorder in the circulation between liver and kidneys, pancreas and kidneys, and will relieve these tensions from the desire for sweets.

3386–2

10. Milk

For milk, whether it is the dry or the pasteurized or raw, is near to the perfect combination of forces for the human consumption.

1703–2

. . . well that the general strength be builded up with beef juices, eggs, and milk drinks, and the easily assimilated foods.

265–9

11. Mummy Food

This special recipe for "mummy food" was given to Cayce in a dream nearly fifty years ago. He asked about it in a reading and the same experience took place. The mummy in the dream came to life and translated ancient Egyptian records for him; then gave him the recipe and told him it was a "spiritual" food (see page 245 for recipe).

12. Potato Peelings

Q-4: What foods or treatments are especially good for bringing more of the luster—reds, coppers, and golds—back into the hair?
A-4: Nothing better than the peelings of Irish potatoes or the juices from same. Don't just put the peelings in water and cook them, because most of the necessary properties will go out, but put them in Patapar paper to cook them.

2072–14

Q-10: Suggest diet beneficial to preserving teeth.
A-10: Eggs, potato peelings, seafoods—all of these are particularly given to preserving the teeth; or anything that carries quantities of calcium or aids to the thyroids in its production would be beneficial—so it is not overbalanced, see?

1523–3

13. Spiritual Food

Q-27: Spiritual foods?
A-27: These are needed by the body just as the body needs fuel in the diet. The body mental and spiritual needs spiritual food—prayer, meditation, thinking upon spiritual things. For thy body is indeed the temple of the living God. Treat it as such, physically and mentally.

4008–1

14. Water

And, above all, drink plenty of water every day, that there may be a flushing of the kidneys, so that the uric acid and the poisons that have been as accumulations may be removed.

2273–1

Do not drink water with meals. Take the water between the periods, see?

5647–1

Q-8: How much water is necessary for drinking?
A-8: All the body may drink; six to eight ounces taken three to four times each day.

850–3

15. Wine

. . . for as we find RED WINE would be excellent if taken as a meal with black or sour bread, in the evenings or late afternoon.

437–7

A stimulation occasionally as of wine with bread, not as a drink but just as a potion to bring rest to the body. When taken it should only be with rye or sour or brown bread.

846–1

No beer, no strong drink; though red wine as a *food* may be taken occasionally—for this is blood building and blood-resisting forces are carried in same—as iron and those plasms that make for the proper activity upon the system. But never more than two or two and a half ounces of same, but this only with black or brown bread, and not with sweets.

1308-1

. . . wine taken in excess—of course—is harmful; wine taken with bread alone is body, blood and nerve and brain building.

821-1

16. Yogurt

Also we would add yogurt in the diet as an active cleanser through the colon and intestinal system. This would be most beneficial, not only purifying the alimentary canal, but adding the vital forces necessary to enable those portions of the system to function in the nearer normal manner.

Thus we may bring the abilities for strength and for purifying the circulatory forces, upon which depends the strength to resist physically the inroads of the infectious forces that disturb the locomotion as well as the pulmonary and the circulatory system and the strength through the depleting of the nerve energies of the body.

1542-1

8

--- ❋ ---

Seventeen Days in the Temple Beautiful

THE LEGEND

Many thousands of years ago in Egypt—and perhaps also in Atlantis—there existed a Temple Beautiful and a Temple of Sacrifice. When I visited Cairo several years ago, our guide took us to a place in front of the sphinx and told us the story of how that lion with a man's head was found in the sand long ago by a man who dreamed it was there. Then the guide turned and pointed to a place to his right and said, "And that's where the Temple Beautiful once stood." He didn't elaborate on the story, but the legend had passed down from one generation to the next—and there it was.

The story of the Temple Beautiful comes into focus most vividly through the Edgar Cayce readings. The subject cropped up time after time, and the story was always the same. It was a place where people came and lived for a time, undergoing purification rites, in a sense, to prepare them to be able to serve better.

These individuals took part in exercises, meditation experiences, used music and dance to expand their consciousnesses, and were given foods specially chosen and prepared.

Even the building itself was uniquely constructed, being in the form of an egg—on end, set one-third of its length into the earth—situated within a pyramid. It looks something like this:

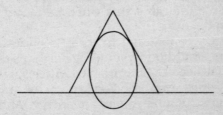

Both of these forms have acquired mystical significance over the ages. It is from the egg, of course, that life comes in the chicken. The shape of the egg gives it exceptional strength. Did you know that most people cannot crush an egg in one hand simply by squeezing? (No rings allowed, of course.) I've tried it myself, but I don't know if it's been done with a professional football linebacker. In any event, I tried hard, holding my hand over the kitchen sink, but the egg remained intact.

The pyramid, of course, has had millions of words written about it throughout the centuries. It has been suggested that the pyramid foretells the future, even to the present day. Books have been written about the energies within the pyramid, and small replicas of this structure, oriented properly to magnetic worth, apparently give preservative powers to objects set in the center within the structure.

Both the egg and the pyramid are symbols in the unconscious minds of people throughout the world. Symbology is called the language of the unconscious. And it is here, in the unconscious, that we receive messages in dreams and visions. The Temple Beautiful, then, in its original state, was surrounded by the mystical, as were its teachings. Cayce indicated this when he talked about those experiences.

The Cayce material in itself is mystical and points us toward understanding ourselves as mysteries that need to be unraveled. After all, we *are* energy beings, composed—all of us—of atoms as our basic structure. Atoms are energy. And, also from the Cayce readings, we are given the concept that each atom has consciousness. This may be difficult to understand; but then, if we are mysteries to be understood, it stands to reason that there is much of us that is as yet not explained.

From the material on the Temple Beautiful, we are told that music is one of the greater means of reaching the depths of our unconscious minds, where memories reside of past lifetimes on the Earth. And some say it is with music and mathematics that the universes were created. Here is one quote about music that stimulates our imagination:

> For, hath it not been said that only music may span that space between the finite and the infinite? The entity's music may be the means of arousing and awakening the best of hope, the best of desire,

the best in the heart and soul of those
who will and do listen. Is not music the
universal language, both for those who
would give praise and those who are sorry
in their hearts and souls? Is it not a
means, a manner of universal expres-
sion? Thus, may the greater hope come.

2156–1

The Temple Beautiful can be looked at as a
symbol of the body itself, and the cleansing and
purification that took place there may have been
the message from the Creative Forces that such a
process must come into our own bodies in one way
or another. And, really, the ways and manners
have been rather clearly identified over the ages
and are available for us to put into action now.

One of the ways in which a person's body may
be made more "spiritual," according to the Cayce
story, is a food that was described to Edgar in a
dream. His dream concerned the discovery of ancient records in Egypt. A mummy in the dream
came to life and helped him translate these records. She described to him the kind of food she
needed to stay alive. It was called "Mummy Food"
subsequently, and later on was described in the
readings as spiritually beneficial for the body. One
of the readings gave this information:

. . . and for this especial body, a mixture
of dates and figs that are dried, cooked
with a little cornmeal—a very little sprinkled in—then this taken with milk,
should be almost a spiritual food for the
body.

275–46

173

You'll find the recipe, which has worked well for many, in the material in Chapter 9.

We find in the Christian Bible that we are indeed the Temple of the Living God. We need to bring about a cleansing—and then the awareness of the Divine will grow into more of a reality—for God does dwell within:

> Realize then, ever, that thy body is indeed the tabernacle, the temple of the Living God. That which ye may comprehend of Him is everpresent.
>
> 2900–2

> Thy body is indeed the temple of the living God. Hold to that. By might and main of the mind, attempt to make the best, the most beautiful, the most acceptable temple according to thy concept of a living Christ Consciousness. Hold to that. Let no one, in any manner, take that from you.
>
> Then apply, in an expectant manner, those measures which will aid the body-forces to create within self those influences necessary for this building of the body to a beautiful temple to thy God.
>
> The world and the earth, and all that is in it, are the Lord's. Use those forces, then, in physics, in pathology, in *all* forces pertaining to the body building.
>
> 2968–1

And we might well say, let's use those things that we take into our bodies as food, in a like manner—as of Divine origin. In that way, the best will come about, and this Temple Beautiful that we know as our body will thrive. Our consciousness will expand, and the world will feel the difference, even though it be only bit by bit.

It was in 1978 that we put into action an idea that had been germinating for quite a while: Why not establish a Temple Beautiful Program at the A.R.E. Clinic? Use the concepts that were used thousands of years ago, and add to them what we know about energies, about the mind, about the use of music—and about food and its selection and preparation?

We started such a program, obtained a building that looked the part, and designed the event to last seventeen days. Much work went into the formulation of the program, but efforts were made to pay attention to the development and realization of all aspects of the human being—the spiritual reality, the building aspects of the mind, and the needs of the ailing human body.

Thus there came into reality regular periods of meditation; opportunities with music to gain insights into the unconscious mind; group therapy; counseling; dream recall and interpretation; all the physical kinds of therapy-massage, manipulation, hydrotherapy, and colonics; and, more recently, electromagnetic field therapy. Then there are those periods of instruction in healing, dreams, biofeedback, and the practical application of nutrition—the use of foods to help bring the body back to its normal condition of balance.

All of this came about from the foundation of the medical practice that had been established at the clinic from its beginning in 1970.

As we progressed through dozens of these programs, it became evident that those who have gone through the seventeen days have been deeply interested in the diet they had been following. The menu for the program became more and more refined and usable.

It was for this reason I felt it was important that we include in this book a menu we use for the entire seventeen days and the recipes that back it up. There are other recipes in that section of the book (Chapter 9), but all those that are used in the Temple Beautiful Program are included.

Many of our patients who go through the program are on a special diet. These are observed and given individual attention. The menu for the seventeen days, however, is that which is served the majority of the participants in the program, for it follows—as much as we can make it—the concepts in the Cayce material about what is a good, balanced diet, one that will help the body in a beneficial, constructive manner.

Certain rules follow throughout the program. We use no white sugar, no white flour, have no fried foods, and eliminate both pork and beef from the foods offered the participants. The entrée for each evening meal is alternated between either a fish or fowl dish one night and a vegetarian dish the next. Baked apples are used occasionally at breakfast time, but never raw apples. Fruits are offered at breakfast, salads at lunch, and the two are never combined. Coffee is available for those who wish it, but it is strongly recommended that neither milk, cream, or sugar is added to the coffee. All breads are whole wheat sweetened with fructose, honey, or corn syrup—all butter must be unsalted. All cereals and pancake mixes require the stone-buhr brand.

Teas are available at each meal. These are a variety of herbal teas—including chaparral, pau d'arco, and Jason Winters—and those that may be especially recommended by the patient's doctor, or usually a part of the patient's diet. These, with the coffee, offer a choice of beverages for individual tastes, needs, and desires.

Fruits and fruit juices—a variety of each, especially the fruits that are in season—are offered at each breakfast time. And at lunch there are available a choice of three or four different dressings for the salad that is always served at lunchtime. Almost without exception, both salad and soup form the basis for lunch.

Individually designed diets are arranged according to the needs of those whose illness calls for them. Those patients who are trying to overcome cancer, hypoglycemia, candidiasis, multiple sclerosis, diabetes, or any of those conditions mentioned in Chapter 6 adapt the basic diet to their needs and end up with a special dietary intake, always with assistance and direction.

Throughout the seventeen days of meals, there are certain items marked with an asterisk. These will be found in the recipes identified in Chapter 9. Those without an asterisk are not in need of a recipe, but may require a bit of your own creativity. Have fun with your use of these bits of commonsense eating.

SEVENTEEN DAYS OF MENUS

DAY

1

Breakfast not served today. Program participants arrive during the morning or early afternoon hours.

LUNCH

Fresh green salad with lettuce, sliced avocado, sliced cucumbers, and sliced tomatoes (choice of *Lemon Vinaigrette Dressing, *Buttermilk Dressing, or *Poppy Seed Dressing)
*Confetti Soup
Assorted Whole Wheat Crackers and platter of assorted cheeses
Coffee or herbal teas

DINNER

Relish platter of carrot sticks, cucumber slices, radishes and black olives
*Mushroom Chicken
*Pimiento Green Beans
*Squash Medley
Coffee or herbal teas

SNACK/DESSERT

*Orange Gelatin Dessert

DAY

2

BREAKFAST

Fruit, grape juice, and white grape juice

Stone-buhr Hot Apple Granola, milk

Honey, whole wheat, cinnamon or raisin toast
    with unsalted butter, or rice cakes (toppings:
    raw almond butter, peanut butter, strawberry
    jam, plum jam, raw almonds, or raisins

Coffee, cinnamon-rose tea, pau d'arco tea

Sliced bananas with cherry garnish, or diced pears
    with kiwi garnish

LUNCH

Fresh green salad with lettuce, shredded red cab-
    bage, chopped celery, shredded carrots, and
    black olives (choice of dressing)

*June's Chicken Soup

Assorted whole wheat crackers, or rice cakes (top-
    ping: almond butter)

Coffee or herbal teas

DINNER

Platter of sliced tomatoes, sliced avocados, jicama
    sticks, and black olives

*Dr. Gladys's Green Chili Quiche

*Lemon Broccoli

*Scallion Carrots

*Corn Bread with unsalted butter

Coffee or herbal teas

SNACK/DESSERT

*Strawberry Mousse

DAY
3

BREAKFAST

Grapefruit with cherry garnish, or choice of other juices

Plain scrambled eggs, or scrambled eggs topped with Tillamook cheese and, served with diced green onions, diced tomatoes, and salsa

Rice cakes, or buttered cinnamon-raisin toast with unsalted butter.

Raw almond butter, plum jam, or apricot-pineapple jam—raw almonds or raisins.

Coffee, or cinnamon-rose tea, or pau d'arco tea

LUNCH

*Mexican Bean Salad
*Dilly Tuna Salad
*Sunburst Broccoli with *Lemon Mayonnaise
Platter of lettuce, tomatoes, avocados, and black olives
Whole grain rye and whole wheat breads
Coffee or herbal teas

DINNER

*Paprika Fillet of Fish with *Lemon Pickle Sauce
Fresh green salad with lettuce, chopped green pepper, zucchini julienne, and sliced radishes (choice of dressing)
*Lima Beans with Scallions
*Spiced Cabbage
Coffee or herbal teas

SNACK/DESSERT

*Raspberry Pears

DAY
4

BREAKFAST

Fruit and juices
Fresh Fruit with kiwi garnish
French toast with Vermont maple syrup, unsalted
    butter
*Mummy Food
Raw almond and peanut butters, jams
Raw almonds or raisins
Coffee, pau d'arco tea, or country apple tea

LUNCH

Fresh green salad with lettuce, spinach, chopped
    celery, sliced cucumbers, chopped green on-
    ion, and red peppers (choice of dressing)
*Cream of Cauliflower Soup
Coffee or herbal teas

DINNER

Relish platter of carrot sticks, celery sticks, green
    onion, sliced cucumbers, and black olives
*June's Nut Loaf with *Tomato Sauce I
*Pimiento Peas
*Parslied Cauliflower
Coffee or herbal teas

SNACK/DESSERT

Fresh Fruit

DAY
5

BREAKFAST

Selection of fruit and juices
Sliced bananas, fresh applesauce with mint leaf
    garnish
Cream of Rye cereal with skim milk
Cinnamon-raisin toast, wheat and honey toast, or
    cracked wheat toast with unsalted butter, or
    rice cakes
Raw almond and peanut butters, jams
Raw almonds or raisins
Coffee, herbal teas, or pau d'arco tea

LUNCH

Fresh green salad with lettuce, sliced tomatoes,
    sliced avocado, chopped jicama, black olives
    (choice of dressing)
*Chili Lentil Soup
*Chili-Chili Cornbread with butter
Coffee or herbal teas

DINNER

Relish platter of green pepper strips, cauliflower
    florets, tomato wedges, and black olives
*Southwestern Barbecued Chicken
*Gypsy Stir-Fry
*Lemon-Dilled Brussels Sprouts
Coffee or herbal teas

SNACK/DESSERT

*Creamy Banana Delight

DAY
6

BREAKFAST

Orange, grapes, and kiwi—pineapple with mint leaf garnish

Grape juice, apple juice

Plain scrambled eggs, or scrambled eggs topped with Tillamook cheese and diced green onions, and diced tomatoes, and mild or medium salsa.

Toasted cinnamon-raisin bread, honey, whole wheat bread, rice cakes

Almond and peanut butters, jam, raw almonds, raisins

Raw almonds and raisins

Coffee or herbal teas

LUNCH

*Country Garden Soup
*Tofu Sprout Sandwiches
Coffee or herbal teas

DINNER

Fresh green salad with lettuce, shredded red cabbage, sliced cucumber, and sliced radishes (choice of dressing)

*Spaghetti Squash Italiano
*Artichokes Vinaigrette with *Lemon Mayonnaise
*Pimiento Broccoli
Coffee or herbal teas

SNACK/DESSERT

*Banana Cereal Cake

183

DAY
7

BREAKFAST

Yogurt and blueberries
Grape juice
Buckwheat pancakes with unsalted butter and
   Vermont maple syrup, or rice cakes
Raw almond butter, peanut butter, jams, whipped
   Neufchâtel spread
Raw almonds or raisins
Coffee, chaparral tea, pau d'arco tea, country ap-
   ple, mullein, and Haussmann's

LUNCH

Fresh green salad with lettuce, spinach, chopped
   green pepper, sliced cucumber, alfalfa
   sprouts, tomato wedges, julienne of yellow
   squash, and zucchini (choice of dressing)
*Potato Soup with Creamed Vegetables
Assorted whole wheat crackers—rice cakes—butter—almond butter—peanut butter
Coffee or herbal teas

DINNER

Relish platter with carrot sticks, green pepper
   strips, cucumber slices, black olives
*Sautéed Chicken Livers with Onions
*Lemon Peas
*Medley of Greens
Coffee or herbal teas

SNACK/DESSERT

*Citrus Fruit Delight

DAY
8

BREAKFAST

Clear apple juice, or red raspberry juice
Yogurt with blackberries, yogurt with strawberries, or diced pears
*Mummy Food, skim milk
Toast: Light Country, nine-grain, cracked wheat, and rice cakes
Raw almond and peanut butters, jams
Raw almonds or raisins
Coffee, herbal teas (mullein, Haussmann's, chaparral, cinnamon-rose)

LUNCH

*Blender Gazpacho Soup
*Mexican Beans
*Turkey Tacos
*Guacamole
Sour cream—salsa—chips
Coffee or herbal teas

DINNER

Fresh green salad with lettuce, chinese cabbage, spinach, sliced cucumber, julienned zucchini and yellow squash
*Curried Peanut Rice
*Temple Beautiful Eggplant Casserole
*Rutabaga-Carrot Ring
Coffee or herbal teas

SNACK/DESSERT

*Apple Custard

DAY
9

BREAKFAST

Fresh grapefruit, fresh orange juice, or unsweetened apple juice

Choice of strawberries in yogurt or plain quartered
strawberries—raw almonds, raisins

Poached eggs or *Mummy Food

Platter of papaya, pears, and apples with kiwi
garnish

Cinnamon-raisin toast, rice cakes—unsalted butter, raw almond butter, peanut butter, plum
and apricot-pineapple jams

Raw almonds or raisins

Coffee, pau d'arco, mullein, Haussmann's, orange
spice teas

LUNCH

Fresh green salad with lettuce, sliced cucumbers,
shredded red cabbage, and yellow squash
(choice of dressing)

*Split Pea Soup

Rye bread, rice cakes, nut butters

Coffee or herbal teas

SNACK/DESSERT

Cookies made with *Basic Cookie Dough

DINNER

Relish platter with celery sticks, cauliflower buds, radishes, and tomato wedges
*Monastery Fish
Buttered Broccoli
Zucchini & Yellow Squash
Coffee or herbal teas

SNACK/DESSERT

*Banana Nut Ice Cream

DAY
10

BREAKFAST

Apple-pear juice & grape juice

Sliced bananas with cherry garnish, sliced bananas, sliced pears and papaya, raw almonds and raisins

Seven-Grain Cereal

Toast: Wheat & Honey bread, cinnamon-raisin bread and rice cakes

Unsalted butter, raw almond & peanut butters and jams (orange marmalade, strawberry)

Raw almonds or raisins

Coffee, pau d'arco, mullein, chaparral, Haussmann's, country apple

LUNCH

*Italian Garden Salad

*Springtime Egg Salad

Cheese Platter

Avocado-Tomato-Olive Platter

Whole Wheat and Rye Bread

Coffee or herbal teas

DINNER

Fresh green salad with lettuce, spinach, chopped celery, zucchini, and tomato

Roast turkey

Zucchini

Beets

Coffee or herbal teas

SNACK/DESSERT

Watermelon or fruit in season

DAY
11

BREAKFAST

Pear-grape juice or fresh orange juice
Strawberries in yogurt
Buckwheat pancakes with Vermont maple syrup
   or choice of whipped Neufchâtel with honey
Unsalted butter, raw almond and peanut butters,
   jams
Raw almonds or raisins
Coffee—pau d'arco, chapparal, mullein, Hauss-
   mann's, cinnamon-rose teas

LUNCH

*Creamy garden salad
Cold sliced turkey
Assorted breads
*Cranberry mold
Lettuce, cucumber, beets platter
Coffee or herbal teas

DINNER

Fresh green salad with choice of dressing
*Monastery Fish
*Lemon-Dilled Brussels Sprouts
Coffee or herbal teas

SNACK/DESSERT

Fruit and ice cream

DAY
12

BREAKFAST

Fruit & cherry juice, or grapefruit juice
Baked apples with unsalted butter and cinnamon
French toast with maple syrup or choice of honey,
  or rice cakes
Raw almond and peanut butters, jam
Raw almonds and raisins
Coffee, pau d'arco, chaparral, mullein, Hauss-
  mann's, country apple teas

LUNCH

Fresh green salad with choice of dressing
*Russian Borscht
Salmon platter with lemon wedges
Assorted whole grain breads, rice cakes, whole
  wheat crackers
Coffee or herbal teas

DINNER

Relish platter of jicama, green pepper, radishes,
  black olives
*Ranch Pie
Green Beans
Carrots
Coffee or herbal teas

SNACK/DESSERT

Fresh fruit

DAY
13

BREAKFAST

Apple juice or grape juice
Fresh fruit assortment
Four-grain cereal, skim milk, unsalted butter
Cinnamon-raisin toast, cracked wheat toast with
    unsalted butter, or rice cakes
Raw almond and peanut butters, jams
Raw almonds and raisins
Coffee, pau d'arco, chaparral, mullein, Hauss-
    mann's teas

LUNCH

*Kitchen Sink Garden Salad
*Cabbage Head Soup
*Parmesan Pita Bread
Coffee or herbal teas

DINNER

Relish platter of celery, carrots, green pepper, and
    black olives
*Herb Chicken, or *Garlic Lemon Chicken
*Parslied Cauliflower
Peas with pearl onions
Coffee or herbal teas

SNACK/DESSERT

*Creamy Tropical Delight

DAY
14

BREAKFAST

Choice of pears, bananas, strawberries with yogurt

Fresh orange juice, apple juice

Southwest Scrambled Eggs with diced tomatoes, diced green onions, mild and hot salsa

Cinnamon-raisin toast with unsalted butter, or honey and wheat toast, rice cakes

Raw almond and peanut butters, jams

Raw almonds and raisins

Coffee, pau d'arco, mullein, Haussmann's, chaparral, mandarin orange teas

LUNCH

Fresh green salad with lettuce, chopped celery, chopped cauliflower, sliced tomatoes

*Tomato and Green Pepper Soup

*Turkey Salad and *Herb Chicken Platter

Whole wheat crackers

Rice cakes

Coffee or herbal teas

DINNER

Relish platter with radishes, green pepper, jicama, green onion, and black olives

*Summer Lasagna

*Italian Stir-Fry

*Pimiento Broccoli

Coffee or herbal teas

SNACK/DESSERT

*Apple Upside-Down Cake

DAY
15

BREAKFAST

Choice of applesauce, diced pears, sliced bananas,
   pineapple
Pineapple and orange juice
*Mummy Food
Raw almonds or raisins
Coffee, pau d'arco, chaparral, mullein, Hauss-
   mann's, cinnamon-rose teas

LUNCH

*Green Zucchini Soup
Fresh green salad with lettuce, shredded carrots,
   green peppers, and avocado
Assorted whole wheat crackers with nut butter
Coffee or herbal teas

DINNER

Relish platter with celery sticks, radishes, green
   onion, pea pods, and cauliflower
*Orange Lamb Paprika
*Green Beans Almondine
*Orange and Squash Casserole
Coffee or herbal teas

SNACK/DESSERT

*Ricotta Cheesecake with Cherries

DAY
16

BREAKFAST

Pear-grape juice, unsweetened pineapple juice, fresh orange juice

Choice of bananas, pears, kiwi, strawberries, or grapefruit

Poached eggs—Cinnamon-raisin toast, honey wheat toast with unsalted butter

Raw almond butter, peanut butter, jams (plum, apricot-pineapple)

Raw almonds or raisins

Coffee, mullein, Haussmann's, chaparral, orange spice teas

LUNCH

Fresh green salad with lettuce, sliced green onions, sliced cucumbers, tomatoes, and green peppers

*June's Vegetable Soup Especiale

Platter of lamb slices with orange sauce

Assorted whole wheat crackers, rice cakes, nut butter

Coffee or herbal teas

DINNER

EAT OUT LAST FRIDAY NIGHT OF PROGRAM

DAY
————— 17 —————

BREAKFAST

Pear-apple or grape juice
Pears, bananas, kiwi
Hot apple granola with skim milk
Cinnamon-raisin toast, cracked whole toast with
    unsalted butter
Raw almond butter, peanut butter, apricot-pine-
    apple jam, strawberry jam
Raw almonds or raisins
Coffee, pau d'arco, chaparral, mullein, Hauss-
    mann's, country apple teas

9

✳

RECIPES

It's been said that recipes are for those who don't know how to cook, but let's take issue with that. I think recipes are in the nature of guides that show the way so that the creative ability of the cook might be better manifested.

No recipe will be transformed into the final product identically the same by two different cooks. Each person brings into the process his/her own individual creativity, adding perhaps a bit more, taking away something there. Some love the process, some are indifferent to it, adding in that way creative energies that alter the taste, perhaps, or the texture, or the very molecular makeup of the food thus prepared.

In the same manner that when two persons take the same picture with identical cameras one will make of the print a masterpiece and one a snapshot, two cooks will differ.

This should be kept in mind while using the recipes in this chapter. When you are preparing a meal, make it a creative, loving effort, and you will benefit because of the movement of the Creative Forces through you. And, perhaps more importantly, others will eat the food you prepare and it will bless their bodies and be a helpful, healing action in their lives.

The arrangement of the recipes is such that you can locate them easily. They are divided into the seven categories we have listed so that you can make your choices as you need.

PREPARATION TIPS

There are always little things in kitchen technique which make preparation of food easier. Also, some of the suggestions made here need options— for instance, if you don't have a pyrex dish for making a quiche, use a pie crust. When Gladys makes her special quiche at home, she does this, and it has always been a great favorite in our family.

In the great southwest, peppers are not just peppers. There are red, green, and jalapeno chili peppers. You need to be careful, because the red is the mildest, the green relatively hot and the jalapenos are very, very hot. Some of the recipes use chili peppers, and you need to be cautious the first time you attempt such a dish.

You will find a number of brand name foods listed. We have found that these have suited our purposes better than others, and in some instances are nearly irreplaceable. Our purposes, of course, are to make the foods taste best and be most nutritious. Some things, like Knox Gelatin, were mentioned in the readings, which give added importance, in our minds, to their use.

Some cooks have Food Processors. These can be adapted to any recipe. But where such help is not available, the tried and true methods of basic food preparation can be relied upon. And remember that pre-heating the oven needs to be at a higher temperature for metal than for glass pans. In the recipe for Chili-Chili Cornbread, for instance, preheating needs to be 400° for metal, 375° for glass pans.

Another tip. Dr. Bonner's Protein Powder is usually found in health food stores. The powder has a tendency to cake and become very hard; therefore, scrape out several teaspoonfuls, fill the bottle with water, and refrigerate. Then use the liquid for flavoring soups, casseroles, and other dishes, instead of bouillon cubes or crystals.

And, when you want to brush your hot vegetables with butter, it's always wise to keep a cube of butter in its wrapper in the refrigerator to use for this purpose.

198

A word about herbal teas and coffee. We view coffee as a food when taken black (without sugar or cream). And we discourage use of sweeteners or substitutes for cream or milk. Herbal teas, however, present a more complex picture. Herbs have been used therapeutically for centuries throughout the world. The Indians in this country, for instance, have used chapparel tea as a medication for arthritis and for cancer. We select several herbal teas to be used if preferred at mealtime instead of coffee, but the use of herbs as therapy for the ailing body is beyond the scope of this book. If you are interested in researching this subject, there are literally hundreds of books available.

As I mentioned earlier in the book, my strong point is the Cayce readings and how they pertain to the health of the body through what we eat. Thus I would not carry coals to Newcastle or tell a cook how to prepare food. You each have a great deal of creativity, and you undoubtedly—for the most part—take a recipe and make it into something you like or your family will adore. So have at it, and match your skills with June, our health-food gourmet cook. You'll like it!

SALADS AND DRESSINGS

Basic Mayonnaise

1 cup vegetable oil
2 tablespoons lemon juice
1 whole egg

Drop whole egg into blender container or food processor. Add 4 tablespoons oil. Turn on low speed and with motor running *slowly* add the remainder of the oil and the lemon juice. Salt and other seasonings may be added if desired, such as ¼ teapoon dry mustard. For thicker mayonnaise, use 2 egg yolks and with motor running slowly add the 1 cup of oil in a thin, steady stream. Makes about 1¼ cups. **Note:** If mayonnaise does not thicken and emulsify, pour the mixture into a pitcher, add 2 more eggs or egg yolks to blender or processor, and proceed as above.

Broccoli Salad

4 cups chopped cooked broccoli
½ cup finely chopped onion
½ cup lemon mayonnaise

Mix all together, chill, and serve garnished with sliced cooked carrots.

Buttermilk Dressing

Use Hidden Valley Ranch with Bulgarian-style buttermilk and safflower mayonnaise.

Cranberry Mold

> 2 packages Knox gelatin
> 1 cup orange juice
> Juice of 1 lemon
> 1 package fresh or frozen cranberries,
>   thawed
> 1 large orange, quartered and seeded
> 1 cup honey
> 1 cup chopped pecans

Dissolve gelatin in juice. Put into blender container and blend with fruits and honey until finely chopped. Add nuts and flick motor on and off until nuts are coarsely chopped. Pour into six-cup mold. Chill until firm. Serves twelve. **Note:** When cranberries are in season and reasonably priced, they may be frozen in their original packages and kept until fresh cranberries are again available.

Creamy Garden Salad

Mix cooked peas, cooked cauliflower, and cooked green beans with enough *Lemon Mayonnaise* to moisten. Garnish with green onion and parsley.

Dilly Tuna Salad

> 2 (12-ounce) cans solid white tuna
> 6 heaping tablespoons basic
>   mayonnaise
> 3–5 tablespoons lemon juice
> 1 tablespoon dill weed
> 3 stalks celery, chopped
> ½ cup green onion, sliced

Mix all ingredients.

Lemon Mayonnaise

> 1 cup mayonnaise
> 1 teaspoon grated lemon peel
> 2–4 tablespoons lemon juice to thin
>   mayonnaise to sauce consistency

Mix all ingredients.

Lemon Vinaigrette Dressing

> ¼ cup fresh lemon juice
> 3 ounces sunflower or safflower oil
> 3 ounces olive oil
> 1 clove garlic, minced
> 2 tablespoons green onion, minced

Mix all ingredients well. Makes 1 cup.

Poppy Seed Dressing

  10 ounces onion, chopped
  1½ cups water
  16 ounce can Sahadi tahini (sesame
      butter)
  4½ cups safflower oil
  2¼ teaspoons celery seed
  2¼ teaspoons poppy seed
  4 teaspoons dry mustard
  1¼ cups honey
  1½ cups lemon juice
  1½ teaspoons garlic powder

Put onion and water in electric blender container and blend until smooth. Add tahini and blend until smooth. Pour into large bowl and whisk in remaining ingredients. Makes about 3 quarts.

Italian Garden Salad

Mix whatever cooked and raw vegetables are on hand with chopped onion, minced garlic, olive oil, and lemon juice to taste.

Use such vegetables as broccoli, green beans, peas, carrots, celery, zucchini, yellow squash, and green and red peppers.

Kitchen Sink Garden Salad

Lettuce, torn into bite-sized pieces
Spinach
Julienned cucumber and zucchini and
  yellow squash
Sliced radishes
Chopped green pepper
Chopped brussels sprouts
Cut green beans

Toss together and serve with choice of dressings.

Mexican Bean Salad

2 cups dry pinto beans
4 cups water
1 cup chopped sweet red pepper or 1 jar
  pimiento
1 cup chopped celery
1 cup chopped green pepper
1 cup sliced green onion
1 tablespoon finely minced garlic
1 teaspoon oregano
½ teaspoon thyme
¼ cup fresh lemon juice
¼ cup olive oil
1 teaspoon salt

Bring beans and water to boil. Boil for 3 minutes and turn off and soak for 1 hour. Then return to boil and cook until tender (about 1 hour). Mix all ingredients together and chill thoroughly. For a real Mexican flavor, add a handful of chopped cilantro, Chinese parsley, or green coriander.

Springtime Egg Salad

>2 dozen hard-boiled eggs
>1 bunch green onions, chopped
>1 green pepper, chopped
>4 ribs celery, chopped
>1 sweet red pepper (optional)
>Salt to taste
>Mayonnaise to moisten
>Lemon juice to taste

Combine all ingredients and mix well.

Turkey Salad

>4 cups chopped cooked turkey
>1/2 cup sliced green onion
>4 ribs celery, chopped
>Lemon Mayonnaise to moisten

Combine all ingredients and mix well. Mound in the center of a platter and surround with left-over *Herb Chicken* or *Garlic Lemon Chicken*.

VEGETABLES

Artichokes Vinaigrette

Wash and trim four to six artichokes. Place upside down in large pot of water to cover with 2 tablespoons cider vinegar. Boil until bottoms are easily pierced with a fork (about 45 minutes). Serve with *Lemon Vinaigrette Dressing* and *Lemon Mayonnaise.*

Green Beans Almondine

Steam green beans in basket over boiling water about 7 to 10 minutes, or until crisp tender. Turn into serving dish. Brush lightly with butter and sprinkle with toasted sliced or chopped almonds. Allow 4 ounces per person.

Gypsy Stir-Fry

2 tablespoons vegetable oil
2 pounds acorn squash, quartered, thinly sliced, and pared
2 pounds green beans, cut into 2-inch lengths
1 bunch green onion, sliced thin
2 tablespoons Dr. Bronner's Protein Powder, diluted with water to taste
1½ cups water
2 ounces diced pimientos
2 teaspoons crumbled leaf marjoram

Heat oil in electric frying pan to 300 degrees. Add squash, stir-fry 5 minutes. Add green beans and stir-fry for 2 minutes. Add remaining ingredients and steam until crisp tender (about 5 minutes). Garnish with parsley sprigs and serve. Serves twelve.

Italian Stir-Fry

3 bunches spinach, chopped
1 bunch beet greens
1 large onion
4 ribs celery, chopped
4 large cloves garlic, minced
4 large yellow squash, julienned
2 tablespoons olive oil

Sauté onion and garlic in oil until limp. Add remaining ingredients and stir-fry until greens are wilted and vegetables crisp tender. Serves twelve to sixteen.

Lemon Broccoli

Place broccoli flowers and stems in steamer basket over boiling water. Steam for about 5 minutes, or until broccoli turns a bright green. Remove flowers to a heated bowl and brush with butter. Garnish with lemon slices. Allow 4 ounces per person.

Peel broccoli stems and slice crosswise for *Sunburst Broccoli.*

Lemon-Dilled Brussels Sprouts

> *2 pounds frozen brussels sprouts*
> *1 cup tiny frozen onions*
> *Juice of ½ medium lemon*
> *Butter*
> *Dill weed and diced pimiento*

Steam brussels sprouts and onions according to package directions (about 5 minutes). Drain. Brush lightly with butter. Add lemon, sprinkle with dill, and garnish with pimiento.

Lemon Peas

Steam 2 pounds tiny peas until tender (about 7 minutes). Brush lightly with butter. Garnish with lemon peel and paprika. Serves twelve.

Lima Beans with Scallions

> *2 pounds frozen baby lima beans*
> *½ cup sliced scallions*
> *Dr. Bronner's Protein Powder*
> *1 tablespoon butter*
> *Parsley*

Cook lima beans according to package directions along with protein powder to taste. When tender, add scallions and butter. Mix well and garnish with parsley.

Medley of Greens

2 tablespoons vegetable oil
2 tablespoons chopped fresh spinach
1 bunch beet greens, chopped
1 bunch bok choy, chopped
1 fresh red bell pepper or 1 jar roasted
    red peppers, chopped
2 large cloves garlic, minced

Sauté all ingredients in vegetable oil until tender. Serves twelve.

Orange and Squash Casserole

1 butternut squash
2 large oranges
1 tablespoon butter

Halve butternut squash, scoop out seeds, slice, and peel. Cube and place in a deep covered casserole dish. Grate peel of 1 or 2 large oranges, then squeeze juice from oranges. Mix squash with grated peel and juice. Bake until tender (about 45 minutes to 1 hour). Add a small amount of butter and serve. Allow 6 to 8 ounces per person.

Parslied Cauliflower

Steam cauliflower florets about 5 minutes, or until crisp tender. Brush lightly with butter. Garnish with parsley.

Pimiento Broccoli

Steam broccoli until barely tender (about 5 minutes). Brush lightly with butter and sprinkle with diced pimiento.

Pimiento Green Beans

Place green beans in steamer basket over boiling water. Steam for 5 to 10 minutes, or until just crisp tender. Remove to serving dish. Brush lightly with butter and garnish with diced pimientos. Allow 4 ounces vegetables per person.

Pimiento Peas

Cook frozen petite peas according to package directions. Brush lightly with butter. Garnish with diced pimiento.

Rutabaga-Carrot Ring or Mold

1 pound carrots, diced
1 pound rutabaga, diced
1 bunch green onions, sliced
1 cup minced parsley
4 tablespoons butter

Steam carrots and rutabaga until crisp tender (about 5 to 7 minutes). Mix with remaining ingredients. Turn into mold and bake at 350 degrees for 30 minutes. Garnish with parsley. Serves twelve.

Scallion Carrots

Steam carrots over boiling water until barely tender (about 5 minutes). Brush lightly with butter and sprinkle with sliced scallions. Allow 4 ounces per person.

Spiced Cabbage

1 large onion, chopped
1 tablespoon garlic, minced
1 large red bell pepper, chopped
1 large head of cabbage, shredded
2 tablespoons olive oil

Sauté onions, garlic, and peppers in olive oil. Add cabbage and cook until wilted and tender.

Squash Medley

Place a combination of sliced zucchini and sliced yellow squash in steamer basket over boiling water. Steam for 3 to 5 minutes, or until barely crisp tender. They should turn a beautiful bright color and still be crunchy when eaten. Remove to serving dish and brush lightly with butter. Allow 4 ounces of uncooked squash per person.

Sunburst Broccoli

> 4 cups chopped steamed broccoli stems
>   and flowers (reserve some flowers
>   for garnish)
> 1 cup chopped celery
> 1 bunch scallions (white portion only),
>   sliced
> 2 cups lightly steamed carrots
> Lemon Mayonnaise

Mix broccoli, celery, and scallions with enough mayonnaise to moisten. Mound in the center of a large round serving plate. Surround with carrots.

MAIN DISHES

Curried Peanut Rice

2 cups raw brown rice, cooked
    according to package directions
1 cup chopped green onion
1 cup chopped parsley
1½ cups toasted chopped peanuts or
    chopped or sliced toasted almonds
4 tablespoons butter
¼ teaspoon salt
1–2 teaspoons curry

Mix all ingredients together while rice is hot.
Serves eight.

Dr. Gladys's Green Chili Quiche

8 ounces chopped green chilies (or
    jalapeño chilies)
2 cups shredded jack cheese
2 cups shredded cheddar cheese
3 cups milk
6 eggs
½ teaspoon coarse sea salt

Grease a 7½-by-12-inch glass casserole.
Spread cheese, then chilies on the bottom. Blend
milk, eggs, and salt. Pour over chili-cheese mixture. This can be used with or without a pie crust.
Bake at 325 degrees for about 45 minutes, or until
knife comes out clean. Serves twelve to sixteen.

Garlic-Lemon Chicken

> 1 large fryer, cut into serving pieces
>   and skinned
> Olive oil for brushing
> Finely minced garlic (about 1
>   tablespoon)
> Salt
> Lemon juice

Brush chicken with oil. Rub with garlic. Sprinkle with salt and lemon juice. Broil until browned, turning as needed. Cover with foil and bake until done (about 30 to 45 minutes).

Herb Chicken

> 2 large fryers cut into serving pieces
>   and skinned
> Olive oil for brushing
> Onion powder
> Garlic powder
> Salt
> 1 teaspoon crushed basil
> ½ teaspoon crushed oregano
> Paprika

Brush with oil. Sprinkle with seasonings. Broil until browned, turning as necessary. Cover with foil and bake until done (about 30 to 45 minutes).

June's Nut Loaf

    1 cup whole wheat bread crumbs
    1 cup chopped celery
    2 cups chopped pecans
    ½ cup chopped parsley
    1 large onion, chopped
    1 large carrot, chopped
    3 eggs
    2 cups milk
    1 teaspoon Spike
    1 teaspoon sea salt
    ¼ teaspoon allspice
    Butter

Chop all vegetables in processor, as well as bread slices for crumbs. Mix all ingredients together. Pour into greased glass loaf pan. Dot with butter. Bake at 325 degrees for 1½ to 2 hours. Turn onto platter and top with tomato sauce. Garnish with parsley and serve. Serves six to eight. **Note:** Bake the nut loaves 1 hour on the upper rack of the oven and the last hour on a lower rack one up from the bottom. Both top and bottom should be nicely browned.

Mexican Beans

4 cups cooked pinto beans
1 medium onion, chopped
1 tablespoon minced garlic
1 stalk celery, chopped
1 medium green pepper, chopped
1 cup tomato sauce
½ cup or more chili sauce
1 tablespoon chili powder
1 teaspoon cumin
Salt to taste
2 quarts water

Simmer together for about 1 hour, pour off excess water.

Monastery Fish

Orange roughy fish fillets (one per
    person)
Lemon slices
Green pepper slices
Onion slices
Salt and pepper

Place fish in a single layer in baking dish. Top with vegetables. Season and dot with butter. Bake at 350 degrees for 15 minutes, or until fish flakes easily.

Mushroom Chicken

3 pounds chicken (organically grown),
    cut into serving pieces and skinned
onion powder
1 can cream of mushroom soup
Blackstrap molasses
Sliced green onion tops

Place chicken pieces in a deep casserole with cover, such as Corning french white oval. Sprinkle with onion powder. Spread with soup. Dribble with molasses in zigzag fashion, using only one to two tablespoons. Spread with a spatula to color the soup. Cover and bake at 350 degrees for about 1 hour. Uncover and bake 20 minutes more, or until nicely browned. Garnish with green onion tops. Serves four.

Orange Lamb Paprika

6 pounds leg of lamb, trimmed of all fat
1½ teaspoons rosemary
1 tablespoon paprika
1 teaspoon salt
2 garlic cloves, minced
½ teaspoon fresh ground black pepper
Orange Basting Sauce
Orange Sauce

Grind all seasonings together with mortar and pestle. Rub over the surface of the lamb. Place lamb on roasting rack, uncovered in shallow baking pan. Cover bottom of pan with water, and replenish as needed so drippings don't burn. Bake at 350 degrees for 3 hours, or until meat thermometer registers medium-well. After 1 hour of roasting, baste with *Orange Basting Sauce.* Continue basting every 20 minutes until lamb is done. Let lamb sit for 15 minutes before slicing. Arrange slices on a platter, cover with foil, and keep warm while making *Orange Sauce.* Garnish with parsley before serving. Serve *Orange Sauce* separately.

Paprika Fillet of Fish

Using your choice of fish, lay fillets in a single layer in baking pan. Sprinkle with onion powder. Spread with mayonnaise. Cut slices of Tillamook cheese into thin slivers. Place about 4 or 5 of these slivers on each fillet. Sprinkle with Hungarian paprika. Bake at 350 degrees for 15 minutes or until fish flakes easily. Allow 1 fillet per person.

Ranch Pie

2 tablespoons vegetable oil
1 large onion, chopped
3 large cloves garlic, minced
2 medium green peppers, chopped
½–1 cup diced green chilies
1 16-ounce can tomatoes, drained and chopped
20-ounce package frozen corn
1 tablespoon taco seasoning mix
3 cups milk
6 extra-large eggs
4 tablespoons butter
6 tablespoons whole wheat flour

1 teaspoon salt
2 cups shredded cheddar cheese

Sauté vegetables in oil until tender. Add corn, chilies, tomatoes, and seasonings. Simmer until corn is tender. Into blender container put milk, eggs, butter, flour, and salt. Blend until well mixed.

Divide vegetables mixture into two 1½-quart rectangular glass casseroles. Sprinkle with cheese. Divide liquid mixture between the two casseroles. Bake at 325 degrees for about 1 hour, or until knife comes out clean and top is lightly browned. May be kept in warm oven until serving time. Serves twelve to sixteen.

Sautéed Chicken Livers with Onions

4 ounces chicken livers per person
Onion powder
Sea salt
Whole wheat flour
Sliced onions
Vegetable oil for sautéeing
Parsley for garnish

Rinse livers and pat dry. Sprinkle with salt and onion powder. Coat with flour. Brush electric skillet with a thin coating of vegetable oil. Heat to 325 degrees. Place livers in a single layer in pan and brown, turning as needed to brown evenly. Remove to platter and keep warm. Repeat until all livers are cooked. In the same skillet brown onions, adding more oil if necessary. When onions are done, place them around the chicken livers. Garnish with parsley and serve.

Southwestern Barbecue Chicken

> 2 fryers, cut into serving pieces and
>   skinned
> 2 cans tomato sauce or 2 cups Tomato
>   Sauce I
> 1 medium onion, chopped
> 1 large clove garlic, sliced
> 1 rib of celery, sliced
> 2 tablespoons lemon juice
> 2 tablespoons Worcestershire sauce
> 1 tablespoon honey
> 2 teaspoons prepared mustard
> Tabasco to taste (optional)

Blend all sauce ingredients in electric blender until smooth. Place chicken in a single layer in shallow baking pan. Pour sauce over all and bake uncovered in 400-degree oven for about 1 hour, or until chicken is nicely browned. If chicken is browning too quickly, turn oven down to 350 degrees. Serves eight.

Spaghetti Squash Italiano

> 12 pounds spaghetti squash
> 4 cups chopped onion
> 4 cups sliced mushrooms
> 6 cloves garlic, minced
> 6 tablespoons olive oil
> 5 cups chopped fresh tomatoes
> 1 quart ricotta cheese
> 4 cups shredded mozzarella cheese
> 1 teaspoon oregano
> 2 teaspoons basil

2 tablespoons Spike
Grated Parmesan cheese

Halve squash and remove seeds. Place in greased pan cutside down and bake about 1 hour, or until easily pierced with a fork. Squash may also be baked whole until tender (about 1½ to 2 hours). Cool enough to handle. Scoop out pulp.

While squash is baking, sauté onions and garlic in 3 tablespoons olive oil. Remove from pan. Reserve to add to squash pulp. In remaining olive oil sauté tomatoes and mushrooms. Add remaining ingredients, along with squash onion mixture. Spoon into two greased rectangular baking dishes. Sprinkle with Parmesan cheese and bake at 350 degrees about 30 to 40 minutes until lightly browned. Serves twelve to sixteen.

Squash Posh

2 eggs
1 cup mayonnaise
1 cup Parmesan cheese
4 medium-sized zucchini or summer squash

Mix together the eggs, mayonnaise, and Parmesan cheese. Mixture will be grainy, like corn meal.

Slice and cook squash with no water until just past soft. Place squash in casserole and cover with Posh mixture, spreading it to edge of dish. Bake for 35 minutes at 350 degrees until Posh is golden brown. Serves eight.

Summer Lasagna

> 9 nine-inch (medium-sized) zucchini
> 1 quart ricotta cheese
> 4 cups shredded mozzarella cheese
> Grated Parmesan cheese
> Tomato Sauce II

Trim zucchini ends and cut each zucchini lengthwise into three slices. Place slices into two rectangular baking dishes (7½-by-12-inches). Cover and bake at 400 degrees for about 30 minutes. Remove from baking dishes.

Cover bottom of casserole with *Tomato Sauce II*. Place a single layer of zucchini strips (about 7), then a layer of ricotta and of mozzarella (about 2 cups of each). Top with sauce, then another layer or zucchini, more sauce, and Parmesan cheese. Serves twelve to sixteen.

Temple Beautiful Eggplant Casserole

> 2 medium-sized eggplants, diced
> 2 large onions, sliced
> 6 ounces stewed tomatoes
> ½ teaspoon salt (seasoned salt, if
>   desired)
> 1 cup sauteed bread crumbs
> Slices of cheddar cheese

Spread onions over the bottom of the casserole dish, cover with eggplant, then pour stewed tomatoes over eggplant. Sprinkle seasoning liberally, then add sautéed bread crumbs. Cover and bake ½ hour at 350 degrees. Uncover and allow to brown 10 to 15 minutes. If desired, then cover the browned bread crumbs with cheddar cheese and place casserole into the oven again until cheese is melted. Serves twelve average appetites (or six teenagers).

Tofu Sprout Sandwiches

Slices of toasted whole wheat bread
Onion slices sautéed in vegetable oil
Avocado slices, sprinkled with sea salt
    and garlic powder
Mung Bean sprouts
Tofu slices
Lemon Mayonnaise

Assemble sandwiches in order given. Top with homemade *Lemon Mayonnaise* mixed with sliced green onion and grated carrot. Broil until lightly browned.

Turkey Tacos

1 cup chopped onion
2 tablespoons oil
2 pounds raw ground turkey
1 teaspoon cumin
½ teaspoon garlic powder, or sauté 2
    cloves minced garlic with onion
1 cup tomato sauce
3 tablespoons picante sauce
3 tablespoons mild taco sauce
1 tablespoon chili powder

Sauté onion in oil until soft. Add turkey, stir until all the pink color is gone. Add rest of ingredients and simmer 30 minutes. Serve in super-sized taco shells garnished with chopped onion, chopped black olives, chopped tomatoes, shredded cheese, and shredded lettuce. Top with taco sauce or picante sauce.

SOUPS, SAUCES, DIPS, ETC.

Blender Gazpacho Soup

½ cup chopped onion
1 large clove of garlic, sliced
3 cups quartered tomatoes
½ large green pepper, chopped
1 small cucumber, peeled and sliced
1 teaspoon salt
3 tablespoons lemon juice
2 tablespoons olive oil
½ cup water
1 tablespoon picante sauce

Put all ingredients in blender container in the order given. Blend until vegetables are finely chopped. Serve cold in small dishes. Makes 8 to 10 half-cup servings.

Cabbage Head Soup

2 tablespoons olive oil
2 cups chopped onion
1 tablespoon garlic, minced
1 pound frozen baby limas
1 large head cabbage, coarsely
    shredded
12 cups water
Dr. Bronner's Protein Powder to taste

Sauté onions and garlic in oil. Add lima beans, cabbage, water, and seasoning. Bring to a boil, lower heat to simmer. Cook until vegetables are tender. Serves twelve.

Chicken Stock

Place all bony parts, such as necks and backs, in stockpot and cover with water. Add 1 chopped onion, parsley, other vegetable peelings, or chopped carrot and celery tops, if desired, and salt (1 tablespoon to a gallon of water). Bring to a boil and simmer for about 1½ to 2 hours. Strain and refrigerate broth. Remove meat from bones and reserve for soups, casseroles, or other dishes. Discard bones and skin.

Beef Juice

Cut 1 pound round steak (no fat) into ½-inch cubes. Place Mason jar with lid on loosely and set over cloth in pan of water. Simmer 2 to 4 hours, then squeeze juice from meat and refrigerate. Sip 1 teaspoon very slowly several times daily. It can be accompanied by whole wheat crackers.

Chili Lentil Soup

   1 large onion, chopped
   3 large cloves garlic, minced (about 1 tablespoon)
   2 teaspoon chili powder (or more, to taste)
   1 teaspoon cumin seed (or more, to taste)
   2 tablespoons vegetable oil
   1 pound lentils, sorted and washed
   10 cups stock or water
   1 carrot, sliced

2 ribs of celery, sliced
1 teaspoon salt
2 tablespoons soy sauce
1 bay leaf

Sauté onion and garlic in oil with chili powder and cumin. And rest of ingredients. Cook until lentils are soft (about 1 hour). Serves eight to ten.

Confetti Soup

7 tablespoons butter
1 cup carrots, chopped in processor
1 large onion, chopped in processor
2 cups zucchini chopped in processor
2 cups celery, chopped in processor
7 cups chicken stock or water
1 cup half-and-half
Dr. Bronner's Protein Powder to taste

Sauté vegetables in butter until soft. Add stock and protein powder and bring to a boil. Simmer for about 10 minutes. Add half-and-half. Heat through. If soup is not thick enough, add more zucchini. Taste for seasoning. Add more protein powder if necessary. Serves eight. **Note:** For a creamier texture, use 4 tablespoons cornstarch mixed with the half-and-half. Heat until thickened.

Country Garden Soup

1 quart vegetable water saved from
steamed vegetables
2 quarts chicken stock
2 cups chopped onion and 1 tablespoon
minced garlic, sautéed in vegetable
oil
Leftover cooked vegetables (may use 1
cup green beans and mushrooms
and 1 cup brussels sprouts); the
flavor will vary according to the
vegetables used
4 cups zucchini, julienned
1 cup celery, sliced
Dr. Bronner's Protein Powder to taste

Puree cooked vegetables with vegetable water.
Add to chicken broth. Bring to a boil. Add remaining ingredients and simmer until vegetables are crisp tender (about 3 to 5 minutes). Serves twelve to sixteen.

Cream of Cauliflower Soup

8 cups pureed cooked cauliflower
8 cups confetti soup
Half-and-half

Steam cauliflower buds about 7 minutes.
Puree with steaming liquid. Add to confetti soup.
Heat to boiling. Thin with half-and-half. Serves sixteen.

Green Zucchini Soup

> 2 tablespoons vegetable oil
> 1 large onion, chopped finely in
>   processor
> 8 cups cooked green vegetables (such
>   as spinach, broccoli, green beans,
>   or peas), pureed in processor
> 2 cups zucchini, chopped fine in
>   processor
> 12 cups stock
> 1 cup heavy cream
> Dr. Bronner's Protein Powder

Sauté onion in oil until limp. Add vegetables, stock, and protein powder. Heat to boiling. Simmer 10 minutes, or until zucchini is tender. Add cream. Taste for seasoning. Add more protein powder if necessary and serve. If soup is not thick enough, add more zucchini. Serves twelve to sixteen.

Guacamole

> 4 large ripe avocados, peeled and
>   mashed
> 1 large tomato, chopped
> ½ large onion, chopped
> ¼ cup lemon juice
> ½ teaspoon salt
> ½ teaspoon garlic powder
> Picante and green chilies to taste

Mix together all ingredients until well blended.

June's Chicken Soup

This soup is based on the typical French country housewife's soup of the day, which consists of a stock which she makes from leftover scraps of meat and bones, vegetable peelings, trimmings, and whatever else happens to be on hand. It is a good way to use up leftovers and is so versatile that it is seldom ever the same. The French housewife is said to be so frugal she never throws anything away—not even the leftover salad. It too gets thrown into the soup pot. The result is an extremely satisfying and tasty soup that tantalizes both the nose and the tastebuds.

> Leftover cooked chicken
> Dr. Bronner's Protein Powder
> 14 cups chicken stock
> 2 tablespoons vegetable oil
> 2 large onions, chopped
> 2 large cloves garlic, minced
> 1 pound mushrooms, sliced

1 pound fresh green beans, cut
Leftover cooked vegetables (about 3
cups)

Sauté onion, garlic, and mushrooms in oil until limp. Add green beans and stock. Bring to a boil and simmer about 5 to 10 minutes until beans are crispy tender. Add protein powder by the tablespoon until it suits your taste. Add the cooked vegetables and the chicken. Heat through and serve. Serves sixteen.

June's Vegetable Soup Especiale

12 cups stock or water
1 large onion, chopped
3 large cloves garlic, minced
1 pound mushrooms, sliced
2 cups cut asparagus
1 cup chopped celery
1 cup cut green beans
1 cup chopped zucchini
1 cup chopped yellow squash
Chopped parsley
2 tablespoons olive oil
Dr. Bronner's Protein Powder

Sauté onions, garlic, and mushrooms in olive oil until limp. Add remaining vegetables except parsley. Sauté vegetables 5 minutes. Add water and protein powder. Bring to a boil and simmer until vegetables are crisp tender. Sprinkle with parsley. Serves twelve.

Lemon Pickle Sauce

2 cups Lemon Mayonnaise
1/4 cup thinly sliced green onion
1/4 cup chopped dill pickles

Mix well and serve with fish.

Orange Basting Sauce

4 tablespoons butter
2/3 cup frozen orange juice concentrate
6 tablespoons burgundy wine

Simmer together for 10 minutes.

Orange Sauce

Pan juices from cooked lamb
1/4 cup frozen orange juice
2 tablespoons red wine
1/2 teaspoon Worcestershire sauce

Pour pan juices into sauce pan. Add rest of ingredients. Heat to boiling and serve with lamb. Serves eight.

Potato Soup with Creamed Vegetables

> 4 tablespoons butter
> 2 large onions, minced
> 2 large carrots, sliced
> 2 ribs celery, sliced
> 1 large parsnip, cubed
> 2 cups cooked cauliflower buds
> 1 pound frozen tiny peas
> 2 cups cooked chopped broccoli
> 2 potatoes, cubed
> 1 cup vegetable water from steamed
>   vegetables
> 3 cups chicken stock
> Dr. Bronner's Protein Powder
> 1 cup whipping cream

Mince raw vegetables in processor. Simmer in butter for about 10 minutes. Meanwhile mince cauliflower in processor. Add to simmering vegetables along with peas. Bring to a boil and simmer until vegetables are tender. Just before serving, add whipping cream and broccoli. Season to taste with protein powder.

Russian Borscht

> 2 quarts stock
> 2 cups diced potato
> 2 cups diced carrot
> 1 cup diced beets
> 1 cup diced onion
> 1 cup diced celery
> 1 cup chopped green cabbage
> 1 cup canned tomatoes
> 2 cloves garlic, minced
> 1 bay leaf
> 2 teaspoons vegetable salt
> ½ cup chopped parsley
> Tabasco sauce to taste

Cook potatoes, carrots, and beets until just tender. Add onion, celery, and cabbage. Cook until just tender. Add rest of ingredients and simmer for 15 minutes. Serve garnished with a dollop of sour cream. Serves ten.

Split Pea Soup

> 2 pounds split peas, sorted and
>   washed
> 1 large onion, chopped
> 2 large carrots, diced
> 4 ribs celery, diced
> 2 bay leaves
> ½ teaspoon thyme
> 8–10 cups water
> Dr. Bronner's Protein Powder and salt to
>   taste
> 4 tablespoons butter

Combine all ingredients. Bring to a boil. Simmer until peas are soft and easily mashed (about 1½ hours). Add butter. Soup may be thinned with half-and-half if desired.

Tomato and Green Pepper Soup

2 large onions, chopped
4 cups chopped fresh tomatoes
2 large green peppers, chopped
3 large carrots, chopped
½ pound tiny peas
2 tablespoons vegetable oil
12 cups stock or water
Dr. Bronner's Protein Powder to taste

Sauté onions, tomatoes, and green pepper in oil until limp. Add remaining ingredients. Bring to a boil and simmer until carrots and peas are tender.

Tomato Sauce I

1 large onion, chopped
2 tablespoons vegetable oil
1 28-ounce can tomato puree
1 (8-ounce) can tomato sauce
1 rounded teaspoon basil

Sauté onion in oil. Add rest of ingredients. Simmer 30 minutes. Makes about 5 to 6 cups.

Tomato Sauce II

5 cups chopped fresh tomatoes
2 large onions, chopped
3 tablespoons vegetable oil
1 28-ounce can tomato puree
1 (8-ounce) can tomato sauce
1 rounded teaspoon basil

Sauté onions and tomatoes in oil until onions are limp. Add remaining ingredients. Simmer 30 minutes or more.

BREADS

Chili-Chili Cornbread

Preheat oven to 400 degrees.

10 tablespoons butter
2 cups whole wheat flour
2 cups whole grain cornmeal
1 teaspoon flour
2 tablespoons baking powder
1 tablespoon chili powder
1 cup diced green chilies
2 eggs
1¼ cups milk

Mix butter and dry ingredients. Add remaining ingredients and mix until well blended. Pour into large rectangular baking pan or two 8-inch-square baking pans that have been well greased. Bake in preheated oven for 45 minutes to 1 hour, or until lightly browned and knife comes out clean. Serves twelve to sixteen.

Cornbread

1 cup cornmeal
1 cup whole wheat flour
1 tablespoon baking powder
1 teaspoon salt
1 beaten egg
1/3 cup butter
1 cup milk
2 tablespoons honey

Mix dry ingredients with butter until crumbly. Then, while mixing, add the rest of the ingredients. Pour mixture into a greased 8-inch-square pan and bake at 400 degrees for about 25 to 35 minutes, or until top is lightly browned and knife comes out clean.

Parmesan Pita Bread

Pita pockets, quartered
Vegetable oil
Garlic powder
Sesame seeds
Parmesan cheese

Brush pita with oil. Sprinkle with garlic powder, sesame seeds, and Parmesan cheese. Broil until cheese browns lightly. Crisp in warm oven. Allow about one whole pita pocket per person.

DESSERTS

Apple Custard

Sliced apples
8 large eggs
½–1 cup honey (depending on tartness
*   of apple or individual taste)*
1 (18-ounce) carton Yoplait yogurt
2 teaspoons vanilla
1 teaspoon cinnamon
Chopped nuts

Grease 2-quart rectangular glass baking dish. Line dish with sliced apples. Combine remaining ingredients and blend until smooth. Pour over apples. Sprinkle with nuts. Bake at 325 degrees for 45 minutes to 1 hour, or until solid when jiggled. Serves twelve to sixteen.

Apple Upside-Down Cake

Sunflower seeds
Sliced apples
1 recipe of Banana Cereal Cake

Grease one very large baking pan or two smaller rectangular pans. Sprinkle with sunflower seeds. Cover with apple slices. Pour prepared Banana Cake batter over apples. Bake in 350-degree preheated oven for 1½ hours, or until knife in center comes out clean. Sometimes this cake takes 2 hours to bake, depending upon the moisture content of the fruit and the cooked cereal.

Banana Cereal Cake

1 stick butter (8 tablespoons)
2 eggs
4 cups mashed banana
4 cups cooked whole grain cereal such
 as oatmeal, seven-grain, or cream
 of rye
1¼ cups whole wheat flour
1 teaspoon baking soda
2 teaspoons baking powder
1 tablespoon cinnamon

Process all ingredients in order given. Turn into two small rectangular pans about 7½-by-12-inches or one very large baking pan. Serves ten to twelve.

Banana Nut Ice Cream

2 cups mashed bananas (more, if not
 sweet enough)
2 cups whipping cream
1 cup chopped toasted pecans or
 walnuts

Mix all ingredients together and process according to ice cream maker directions.

Basic Cookie Dough

> ¼ cup vegetable oil
> ¼ cup butter
> ½ cup honey or 1 cup mashed banana
> 1 egg
> ¼ teaspoon salt
> 2 cups cooked cereal
> 2 cups whole wheat flour
> 1 teaspoon baking powder
> Flavorings and variations

Process oil, butter, honey or banana, and egg until well blended. Add salt, cereal, flour, and baking powder. Process until just mixed. Add flavorings and stir or fold to combine.

Citrus Fruit Delight

> 3 packages Knox gelatin
> 1 (12-ounce) can frozen apple cider,
>   mixed with water to make 4½ cups
> 1 large can pineapple chunks or tidbits
> 2 cups fresh or frozen strawberries

Dissolve gelatin in 1 cup juice. Add pineapple and simmer 5 minutes. Add to remaining juice water mixture. Pour into mold or dish. Add strawberries. Chill until firm. Serves ten to twelve.

my Banana Delight

> 3 packages Knox unflavored gelatin
> 6 ounces frozen apple cider thawed,
>   mixed with apple juice to make 4
>   cups (If apple cider is not available,
>   use frozen apple juice)
> 1 pint sour cream
> Sliced bananas
> 1 cup frozen Bing cherries

Dissolve the gelatin in 1 cup of the juices. Cover a large glass rectangular casserole (about 2 quarts) thickly with banana slices. Mix the dissolved gelatin with the juices and sour cream. Pour over the bananas. Dot with cherries and chill until firm. Serves twelve.

Creamy Tropical Delight

Proceed as for *Creamy Banana Delight,* substituting cooked pineapple and fresh or frozen strawberries for bananas and cherries. Coconut may be added if desired.

Fruit and Spice Cookies

> 2 *cups* Basic Cookie Dough
> 1 *cup unsweetened shredded coconut*
> 1 *cup chopped pecans*
> 2 *cups* Mummy Food
> ½ *teaspoon cinnamon*
> 2 *tablespoons fresh lemon juice*
> *Grated peel of medium sized lemon*

Mix all ingredients and drop dough by tea-spoonfuls onto greased cookie sheet. Bake in center of oven (preheated to 325 degrees) for 15 minutes. Makes about 3½ dozen.

Orange Carob Chip Cookies

> 2 *cups* Basic Cookie Dough
> 1 *tablespoon frozen orange juice*
>   *concentrate*
> *Grated peel of 1 large orange*
> ½ *teaspoon vanilla (optional)*
> ¾ *cup sunflower seeds*
> 1 *cup carob chips*

Mix all ingredients and drop by teaspoonfuls onto greased cookie sheet. Flatten if desired. Bake in center of oven (preheated to 325 degrees) for 12 minutes. Makes about 3½ dozen.

Orange Gelatin Dessert

1 can frozen berry juice (your choice)
6–8 peeled oranges sliced and cut in
half
1 quart water
3 packages Knox unflavored gelatin

Soften gelatin in 1 cup water. Heat until dissolved. Add frozen juice and orange slices. Heat to boiling. Simmer 3 minutes. Add rest of water. Pour into 2-quart gelatin mold or large rectangular glass dish. Chill until firm (about 4 hours). Makes twelve to fourteen half-cup servings.

Raspberry Pears

Fill ripe Anjou Pears with honey-sweetened raspberries.

Ricotta Cheesecake with Cherries

1 quart ricotta cheese
4 large eggs
1 cup Bulgarian-style buttermilk or
Yoplait yogurt
¾ cup honey
2 teaspoons vanilla
Juice and rind of ½ lemon
Bing cherries

Blend all ingredients until smooth. Pour into greased 2-quart rectangular glass baking dish. Bake at 325 degrees for about 45 minutes, or until knife comes out clean. Cool and top with cherries.

Strawberry Mousse

> 1 quart fresh or frozen strawberries
> 1 pint whipping cream
> 1 envelope Knox unflavored gelatin
> ½ cup orange juice
> Honey to taste

Soften gelatin in orange juice and dissolve over medium heat, stirring constantly. Remove from heat and set aside.

Crush strawberries. Whip cream and carefully fold strawberries and dissolved gelatin into whipped cream. Sweeten to taste with honey, folding carefully with every tablespoonful and testing. Pour into custard cups and chill. Serves sixteen.

SPECIALTY FOODS

Mummy Food

> 1 cup dried black figs, chopped
> 1 cup pitted dates, chopped
> 2 rounded tablespoons yellow
>   cornmeal
> 2–3 cups water as needed

Simmer for 15 to 30 minutes, stirring frequently. Serve plain or with milk or cream. The amount of cornmeal and water can be adjusted to your taste.

10

Food Isn't Everything,
But . . .

You can see by now that there is no perfect diet that will work for everyone—it depends on the pH factor, the combinations of foods used, the condition of the body as a whole, and the consciousness of the individual for whom the diet is prepared.

Some years ago I was caring for a woman who had been anemic for a long time. I had given her an iron medication for a period of three months but her hemoglobin remained at about 9.3 grams. She was on the same diet that she had been on, and I was not too well-informed about nutrition in those years. But she had no sign of internal pathology.

She had developed an allergy to the iron, which brought on a skin rash. So I stopped the iron therapy. Since I had read in my research on castor oil as a therapy in the human body that castor oil internally was used by a dermatologist in the thirties for severe skin rashes, I asked the woman if she minded taking castor oil orally. She didn't—she had taken it as a child, and had never minded it. I instructed her to take an ounce at once, then repeat it in four days.

She returned six weeks later, feeling great. She had taken an ounce of the castor oil every four days, not understanding my directions! I checked her iron, and her hemoglobin was up to 13.5 grams, which is very normal for a woman her age.

The story, funny in one regard, demonstrates how the cells of the lining of the upper intestinal tract can be cleansed and can change the manner in which the body functions. Now, after cleansing, the assimilation of foods was more normal and the iron could be gained for the woman's body from her normal diet. The condition of her body as a whole was the major factor here in the utilization of the food she was already eating.

As far as your own diet is concerned, some of the same results can be anticipated that this woman experienced, for the proper diet will aid those forces of assimilation that bring the needed vitamins and minerals into the body in their best form.

By availing yourself of the information offered in these pages and making up a new set of eating—and living—habits, you can move toward a better state of health and an even greater expectancy of longevity.

But I think it is always wise to look beyond simply a diet and always keep in mind there are other things happening in our bodies that deal with a higher concept of what we really are. The electrical nature of how we function, for instance, is always with us. Every thought, every movement, is brought on or made possible by electrical activity of the very fine, low vibratory nature of that which passes through our tissues—through our nervous system.

Cayce explained it this way:

> . . . For as the very forces of the bodily functioning are electrical in their activity, the very action of assimilation and distribution of assimilated forces is in the physical body an active force of the very LOW yet very high VIBRATORY forces themselves.
>
> 470–22

And we must remember, too, that we are individuals who have a higher destiny than seems apparent most of the time, and we need to keep that destiny (and our origin) in mind as we prepare food, as we eat the food, and as we might instruct our bodies how to use the food—the activity of our minds on the functioning of our bodies. This keeps problems from arising when they might otherwise do so. Another of the Cayce suggestions deals with this:

> . . . But if the body is fed only upon that which is temporal in its concept, in its activity, then it MUST of itself become a burden sooner or later . . .
>
> 1691–1

WHAT ELSE CAN YOU DO?

1. Learn to Grow Your Own Food

Not everyone can be a complete farmer, growing totally all that he or she might need to eat, but it would be well for everyone who is in the least interested in what his or her diet is going to be to grow *something*.

You may be in a situation where you have no earth anywhere in your living area—living in an apartment, for instance. You can still grow some of your herbs inside in planters, and perhaps can trade herbs for lettuce or carrots or such with someone who has the place where he or she can grow foods.

In our own situations, we find we cannot grow vegetables since our schedule is hectic and we are often away from home. But we can grow trees—they don't require such close attention. And we do: orange, grapefruit, peach, apricot, plum, fig, and olive trees are all alive and well on our property.

Cayce had much to say about organic farming, too much to begin to quote here. He suggested, however, that everyone should be able to grow some of those things that are necessary to his or her life and welfre. The following quotes tell this story pretty well:

> . . . But each individual should be able—by the grace of the divine—to create or build or supply those things for material sustenance. Hence this should be the idea and ideal of every individual; not only be-

cause of the general economic conditions as may become existent in this present land, but because each individual in itself needs the sustaining forces from nature. So does the INFLUENCE of the union of the spirit of such bring a universal consciousness for not only trust in, but the application of that trust to the daily life and experience.

1100–31

. . . This should be the aim, the desire of every soul; to be at least to some extent SELF-sustaining or owning and creating that as ye consume—from GOD's storehouse and soil! Own such.

2345–1

2. Learn More About Sprouts, Herbs, Wheat Grass, and Survival Foods and Their Storage

These subjects were not intended to be dealt with in this book, but much information is available for those who are interested. You can find these things in some of the books in the BIBLIOGRAPHY section I have prepared in the back of this book, but if that is not sufficient, look and ask in the natural food store outlets.

Sprouts are dealt with very adequately in the book *Edgar Cayce on Diet and Health*—a good reference. Other recipes are to be found there, too, which are well tested and tasty.

3. Learn More About Weight Loss

Losing weight is always a difficult thing, for our appetites are so strong and we slip back into old eating habits so easily. Sometimes, too, we have chosen a family heritage that is replete with obesity. The genetic pattern is difficult to get away from, but it can, in reality, be overcome. It does take time, effort, persistence, consistency, and patience.

The reference book *Beyond Dieting* (Cochran, 1983) has further tips and assistance in the adventure that is always associated with losing weight.

4. Search for Other Recipes

Searching for other recipes is a good idea, but always be careful to look at the ingredients and choose those that are health producing: foods that combine well; that follow the 4:1 ratio of alkaline to acid-producing foods; and a vegetable balance of two or three of those grown above the ground to one of those grown below the ground. This will help add to your New Age Kitchen card index of good recipes, which you can be sure will make for a healthier body for you and your loved ones—or for whomever you may be preparing meals.

5. Do More Reading and Studying

It is always important to continue the study. Keep on reading and keep on adding new thoughts and ideas to your information about nutrition and what to you is a commonsense diet.

The first step to take is to look at the BIBLIOGRAPHY section at the end of this book and start your reading there. Much can be gained by studying those books.

The second step is to study the subject of

guided imagery and visualization. Using these techniques, you can lose weight, better achieve body balance, and obtain guidance and promote regeneration of your own body.

At Virginia Beach, there are more than fourteen thousand readings Cayce gave during his lifetime, which are open to the public to read and study. The Association for Research and Enlightenment (A.R.E.) has also prepared, for its membership, groups of readings and some medical commentaries covering a variety of subjects. These are called *circulating files,* and information there includes diets and suggestions about nutrition that add to one's perspective as to what is the best diet for you to follow. (For information, write to A.R.E. P.O. Box 595, Virginia Beach, VA 23451.)

6. Record Your Dreams and Learn to Meditate

Dreams never become really important for anyone until they are recorded—actually written down, and over a period of time. The unconscious mind is like a teacher: If you don't pay attention, the teacher will assume you are not really interested, and you'll get little or nothing from the dream self.

When you start the process, however, of regularly recording your dreams, the development of your psychic or soul self really begins in earnest. The unconscious begins to open itself to the conscious mind and you begin to see glimpses of past life experiences; you may get warnings about something that is likely to happen in the future; you may receive guidance about puzzling situations you find yourself in; you may receive guidance about personal relationships; you may get help in solving financial problems; and you may catch actual glimpses of how you might aid a friend or loved one. All this in addition to the information you might gain about the diet you are using at any given time.

Get a spiral notebook, for example, and have it at your bedside with a pen so that, when you awaken in the morning, you can write down whatever you remember that you would call a dream or a near-dream experience. That will get you started. Then you can read the many books available on the subject and become your own dream interpreter.

Meditation is the other part of the prayer activity. Everyone needs to use meditation as a part of his or her daily activity. Meditation will make the unity of body, mind, and spirit more of a reality and will always aid in the healing process, as it aids in the manner in which food is taken into the human body and utilized.

THE COMMONSENSE APPROACH

Common sense is, in one manner of speaking, the distilled result in your mind of what has been constructive in your life's experiences over the years. It is not the result of scientific inquiry, nor what simply comes out of one person's mental gymnastics, but rather is a very firm approach to a subject that has the power behind it of successful application.

Thus, what you get out of this book is a start

on your own voyage to find out how important it is in your own life to adopt a diet—a way of eating—that can truly be called a commonsense approach.

You need to remember to maintain a sense of happiness, both as you prepare food and when you eat it. Not only that, but it is quite important to really love those plants that you are growing in your own backyard garden. The power of the vibration of joy and expectancy makes the plants grow better and produce more in the way of nutritious elements for your health and well-being. Cayce said it in many ways, but this reading talks about constructive activity—which includes both joy and expectation:

> . . . To do good is to think constructively, to think creatively. What is creative, what is constructive, ye may ask? That which never hinders, which never makes for the bringing of any harm to others . . . For thy smile can make the whole day GLAD for many.

> 1206—13

So, as this book draws to a close, I know you will find for yourself a commonsense way of eating if you find for yourself a joy in the life that you live, if you recognize a purpose for yourself and set about pursuing it, and if you just keep on keeping on. Be patient, persistent, and consistent, and your food will taste better, do you more good for the eating of it, and your body will love you more and more every day.

References
for Further Reading

A full bibliography for this book follows, but first I would like to recommend some of the best books from that list for answering your questions and let you know where you might obtain them.

Brett Bolton wrote a book in 1969 called *Edgar Cayce Speaks.* It is a compendium of quotes from the Cayce readings dealing with foodstuffs. All the quotes are taken out of context with the entire reading, but the age, sex, and general diagnosis of the individual who obtained the reading are there.

To get a wide view of almost anything you might want to put into your mouth in the way of food, Brett's book is an excellent source. Two or three of the quotes I have used here came from her book. I wrote the introduction to the book, so I know it well.

When you are looking for other recipes and more information about cooking and food preparation than is found here, you would do well to consult *Edgar Cayce on Diet and Health*, by Read, Ilstrup, and Gammon. This was also published in 1969, and has been reprinted many times.

A third book that I think is an excellent source for those interested in what Cayce had to say about diet—and about healing—would be Raymond Oullette's *Holistic Healing and the Edgar Cayce Readings*. Many direct quotes from the readings are found there, too, for the Cayce material became the central focus of all three of the books I have mentioned.

Any or all of these books, and those also listed in the bibliography, can be obtained through the Cayce Corner at the A.R.E. Clinic, 4018 N. 40th St., Phoenix, AZ 85018; or the A.R.E. Bookstore, P.O. Box 595, Virginia Beach, VA 23451.

Glossary of Terms

1. **ANKYLOSIS:** Abnormal immobility and fixation of a joint due to pathological changes in the joint or its surrounding tissue. If a joint that normally allows movement is fixed and cannot be moved, then it is ankylosed.

2. **ASSIMILATION:** The various processes whereby the products of digestion are converted to the chemical substances of the body tissues, first passing through the lacteals and blood vessels; or the process of transformation of food into living tissue.

3. **ATROPHY:** One meaning is, a wasting due to the lack of nutrition of a particular part of the body. The second meaning is the reduction in size of a structure after it has come to full functional maturity, such as atrophy of the leg after polio or atrophy of a finger after the nerve supply to that finger has been interrupted or atrophy of an extremity in a newborn because of injury or genetic reasons.

4. **COLOSTOMY:** Colostomy is usually understood to be the opening of some part of the colon to the outside through a surgical incision made in the skin and underlying tissues. In medicine a colostomy is a surgical procedure where incision of the colon is made for the purpose of making a more or less permanent fistula between the bowel and the abdominal wall.

5. **DROSSES:** This is a term used in the Edgar Cayce readings meaning waste products or waste matter or refuse as the result of metabolic activity within the physiology of the human body.

6. **ELIMINATION:** In general terminology, this is the removal or excretion of waste products of the body through the skin, the kidneys, the liver and intestinal tract, and the lungs. All of these are eliminatory organs or systems.

7. **MALABSORPTION:** The inadequate absorption of nutrients from the intestinal tract. This may be due to a disease process affecting the intestinal lining, pancreatic insufficiency, or a variety of other causes.

8. **MEGACOLON:** This is an extremely dilated colon and can be caused by any process that simply enlarges and dilates the large bowel chronically. Acute megacolon is seen in certain toxic conditions.

9. **OPTICS:** Optics, in medicine, pertain to the eyes or to the sight. In the Cayce terminology it is another word for the eyes.

10. **PERIARTICULAR:** This describes any tissue surrounding the joint of the body.

11. **PROXIMAL:** Nearest the point of attachment, the center of the body, or point of reference. This is opposed to distal, which means farthest away from.

12. **REGENERATION:** In medicine, this word means repair, regrowth, or restoration of a part, such as tissues of the body. In the Cayce terminology—and also very specifically in medicine—it means restoration of a part back to the state in which it was created originally.

13. **SCLERODERMA:** A progressive disease of the skin involving collagen tissue and resulting in diffuse leathery induration of the skin, frequently followed by atrophy and pigmentation. The localized form is known as morphea. Involvement of internal organs is often the case.

14. **SYNOVIAL:** Pertaining to the synovia, the lubricating fluid of the joints. Synovia is a clear lubricating fluid secreted by the synovial membrane of a joint.

Bibliography

BOLTON, BRETT. *Edgar Cayce Speaks.* Avon Books. The Hearst Corporation. 959 Eighth Avenue, New York, NY 10019. 1969.

CARTER, M. E., McGAREY, W. *Edgar Cayce on Healing.* Warner Books. 75 Rockefeller Plaza, New York, NY 10019. 1969.

COCHRAN, L. *Beyond Dieting.* A.R.E. Press. P.O. Box 595, Virginia Beach, VA 23451. 1983.

EDGAR CAYCE FOUNDATION. *Attitudes.* Vols. 1–4, A.R.E. Press. P.O. Box 595, Virginia Beach, VA 23451. 1974. (Available from Cayce Corner, 4018 N. 40th Street, Phoenix, AZ 85018.)

McGAREY, W. *Edgar Cayce and The Palma Christi.* A.R.E. Press, P.O. Box 595, Virginia Beach, VA 23451. 1970.

McGAREY, W. *The Edgar Cayce Remedies.* Bantam Books. 666 Fifth Avenue, New York, NY 10103. 1983.

McGAREY, W. et al. *Physician's Reference Notebook.* A.R.E. Press. P.O. Box 595, Virginia Beach, VA 23451. 1983.

OULLETTE, R. *Holistic Healing and the Edgar Cayce Readings.* Aero Press. P.O. Box 2091, Fall River, MA 02722. 1980.

READ, A., ILSTRUP C., GAMMON, M. *Edgar Cayce on Diet and Health.* Warner Books. 75 Rockefeller Plaza, New York, NY 10019. 1969.

SNYDER, ARTHUR. *Foods That Preserve the Alkaline Reserve.* Hansen's Publishing. 250 N. Juanita Avenue, Los Angeles, CA 90004. 1972. (Available from Cayce Corner, 4018 N. 40th Street, Phoenix, AZ 85018.)

TIERRA, M. *The Way of Herbs.* Unity Press. Santa Cruz, CA 95065. 1980.

YOGANANDA, PARAMAHANSA. *Autobiography of a Yogi,* 12th ed. Self Realization Fellowship. 3880 San Rafael Avenue, Los Angeles, CA 90065. 1981.

ABOUT THE AUTHOR

DR. WILLIAM MCGAREY received his medical degree in 1947 from the University of Cincinnati College of Medicine. In 1970, he and his wife Gladys Mc-Garey joined the A.R.E. Clinic where they have served as its Directors and primary physicians. They are also former Directors of Medical Research of the Edgar Cayce Foundation. Dr. McGarey is the author of EDGAR CAYCE REMEDIES, EDGAR CAYCE ON HEALING, EDGAR CAYCE'S READINGS ON HOME AND MARRIAGE, EDGAR CAYCE AND THE PALMA CHRISTI, AND HEALING MIRACLES: USING YOUR BODY ENERGIES.

The Edgar Cayce story is one of the most compelling in inspirational literature. Over the course of forty years, "The Sleeping Prophet" would close his eyes, enter an altered state of consciousness, and then speak to the very heart and spirit of mankind on subjects such as health, healing, dreams, meditation, and reincarnation. His more than 14,000 readings are preserved at the Association for Research and Enlightenment.

EXPLORE THE SPIRITUAL WORLD WITH SHIRLEY MacLAINE AND JESS STEARN

Check to see which of these fine titles are missing from your bookshelf:

Titles by Jess Stearn:

☐ 26085   EDGAR CAYCE: SLEEPING PROPHET $4.50

☐ 25150   SOULMATES $3.95

☐ 26057   YOGA, YOUTH, AND REINCARNATION $3.95

Titles by Shirley MacLaine:

☐ 27557   DANCING IN THE LIGHT $4.95

☐ 27370   OUT ON A LIMB $4.95

☐ 27438   "DON'T FALL OFF THE MOUNTAIN" $4.95

☐ 26173   YOU CAN GET THERE FROM HERE $4.95

☐ 27299   IT'S ALL IN THE PLAYING $4.95

☐ 05367   GOING WITHIN $18.95

Look for them in your bookstore or use the coupon below:

Special Offer
Buy a Bantam Book
for only 50¢.

Now you can have Bantam's catalog filled with hundreds of titles plus take advantage of our unique and exciting bonus book offer. A special offer which gives you the opportunity to purchase a Bantam book for only 50¢. Here's how!

By ordering any five books at the regular price per order, you can also choose any other single book listed (up to a $5.95 value) for just 50¢. Some restrictions do apply, but for further details why not send for Bantam's catalog of titles today!

Just send us your name and address and we will send you a catalog!